High Huts of the White Mountains

Second Edition

Nature Walks, Natural History, and Day
Hikes around the AMC's Mountain Hostels

William E. Reifsnyder

with contributions by Ray Welch and
Jan M. Collins

APPALACHIAN MOUNTAIN CLUB BOOKS
BOSTON, MASSACHUSETTS

Nature walks maps by Scott Burns
Book design: Carol Bast Tyler

Distributed by The Talman Company, Inc.

Published by the Appalachian Mountain Club. No part of this publication may be reproduced or transmitted in any form or by any means, electronic or mechanical, including photocopying and recording, or by any information storage or retrieval system, except as may be expressly permitted by the 1976 Copyright Act or in writing from the Publisher. Requests for permission should be addressed in writing to Appalachian Mountain Club Books, 5 Joy St., Boston MA 02108.

Library of Congress Cataloging-in-Publication Data
Reifsnyder, William E.
    High huts of the White Mountains: a history of the Appalachian Mountain Club's New Hampshire mountain hostels / William E. Reifsnyder. — 2nd ed.
        p. cm.
    Includes bibliographical references (p.) and index.
    ISBN 1-878239-20-1 (alk. paper) : $10.95
    1. Mountain shelters—White Mountains (N.H. and Me.)—History. 2. Hiking—White Mountains (N.H. and Me.)—Guidebooks. 3. Trails—White Mountains (N.H. and Me.)—Guidebooks. 4. White Mountains (N.H. and Me.)—Guidebooks. 5. Appalachian Mountain Club. I. Title.
GV199.42W47R45   1993
796.5'22—dc 20
                                                                                        93-972
                                                                                        CIP

The paper used in this publication meets the minimum requirements of the American National Standard for Information Sciences—Permanence of Paper for Printed Library Materials, ANSI Z39.48–1984.∞

**Due to changes in conditions,
use of the information in this book
is at the sole risk of the user.**

✪ Printed on recycled paper.

Printed in the United States of America.

10 9 8 7 6 5 4 3 2 1   93 94 95 96 97

Contents

Acknowledgments

THE information in the pages that follow comes from many sources: hut crews, hut naturalists, various AMC maps and guidebooks, colleagues on the AMC hut committee and its successor committees, and my own mountain wanderings. I have leaned heavily on the encyclopedic knowledge of Joel White, AMC hut system manager from 1975 to 1980. Drs. John Creasy and Charles Burnham read and strengthened the material on the geology of the White Mountains, for which I am grateful. C. Francis Belcher, John Reading, and Bob Daniels also made helpful comments. I am, of course, responsible for the errors and misstatements that remain. To all those who helped, directly or indirectly, I express my deep appreciation.

I would also like to acknowledge the contribution of the AMC education department and the hut naturalists, Ray Welch and Jan M. Collins who developed the self-guided nature walks and gave permission for the reproduction of the descriptive brochures as sidebars in this volume.

The publication staff members who translated the manuscript into a book include Marny Ashburne, Jennifer Yoder, and Gordon Hardy.

Nature walks maps are by Scott Burns.

Please send comments and corrections to Editor, Appalachian Mountain Club Books, 5 Joy Street, Boston, MA 02108.

Introduction

▼

THE story of the high huts of New Hampshire's White Mountains begins before any shelter was built. Mt. Washington, the highest peak of the so-called Presidential Range, had long been a mecca for White Mountain climbers. In 1819 two pioneers, Abel Crawford and his son Ethan, blazed the Crawford Path, which ascends the great mountain from the southwest. Twenty-one years later the trail was converted into a bridle path. By 1861, there was a carriage road up the eastern slopes of Mt. Washington from the Glen House. And in 1869, Sylvester Marsh's dream of a cog railway up the western ridge was realized. It was immediately popular and attracted thousands of tourists who wanted to view the "epic landscape" from the summit. In 1874, more than 10,000 tourists reached the top, 7,000 of them having ridden the open cars pushed by the clanking and snorting engine, Old Peppersass.

But the northern peaks of the White Mountains were reserved for the climbers, hardy men and women who disdained the mechanical means of ascent. They preferred the rugged climb through the deep forests of the northern slopes, across the chain of tundra peaks stretching in a great arc southward from Mt. Madison to culminate at the summit of Washington. It was an arduous trip. Moses F. Sweetser's 1890 edition of *The White Mountains: A Handbook for Travelers* claimed that "this route has been traversed in 12 hours, but there is too much noble scenery along its course to be satisfactorily studied in so short a time. It is therefore wiser to encamp one night along the way. But if the wind is blowing and a storm threatens, it would be unsafe to pass the night on the ridge, and the travelers will be forced to go far down into one of the lateral ravines." With so much exposed ridge to traverse, the journey could indeed be very hazardous.

So the fledgling Appalachian Mountain Club, whose climbers had recently made Randolph to the north a base for their mountain adventures, realized that a secure shelter was needed near timberline in the northern peaks. This would provide not only overnight accommodations for hikers making the long trek to Washington, but also a high base for climbers exploring the northern peaks. A small stone hut, patterned after the huts in the European Alps, was built in the summer of 1888 in the col between Mt. Madison and Mt. Adams. And so, with the construction of Madison Spring Hut, the AMC launched a program of building refuges for walkers in the high mountains of New Hampshire.

The Appalachian Mountain Club had been established in 1876 for the purpose of exploring the mountains of New England and the adjacent regions for both scientific and artistic purposes. To accomplish these goals, the Club set up five departments: natural history, topography, art, exploration, and improvements. In the years since, AMC staff and volunteer members have been building trails, erecting shelters, leading educational hikes and programs, and working to enable lovers of the mountains to explore and enjoy them while at the same time protecting the mountain environment for future generations.

With the construction of the first hut at Madison Spring, the Club laid the foundation for the current string of eight high huts and Pinkham Notch base camp. An emergency refuge high on the Crawford Path, on Bigelow

Lawn, was constructed in 1901 after two experienced climbers perished in a vicious late-June ice storm. This was replaced by a sturdy stone hut at the Lakes of the Clouds in 1915. A stone building was constructed in Carter Notch in 1914 to replace a log cabin that had been there since 1904.

Although these early huts were operated without a caretaker, it soon became evident that an unattended hut was an invitation to vandalism. Wood floors at Madison Spring Hut were ripped up for firewood and, after a few seasons, major construction was necessary. In 1906, an addition was built to house a resident caretaker. From this time on provisions were made in the huts for a hutmaster and eventually for a crew of young "hutmen" to prepare and serve meals. As the number of huts increased, it

The kitchen in Madison Spring Hut in 1911. The telephone was connected in 1906 by a line strung down the mountain to the Ravine House. AMC Collection.

became apparent that an operations base was needed. In 1920 the first buildings at Pinkham Notch were built.

Much of this activity predated the establishment of the White Mountain National Forest, which was made possible by the Weeks Act of 1911. By 1916, the U.S. Forest Service had acquired only 272,000 acres of land, less than half the present size of the forest. The Appalachian Trail (AT), first conceived by Benton MacKaye in 1921, was not completed until 1937, although the first section in New York was marked in 1922. In the White Mountains, the Appalachian Trail followed the network of trails built and maintained by the AMC and was routed to use the existing AMC huts and shelters.

The 1920s saw a rapid expansion of the hut system. Three new huts opened: Greenleaf, Galehead, and Zealand Falls. Old cabins at Lonesome Lake were acquired by the state of New Hampshire and leased to the AMC for operation as a hut. The complex at Pinkham Notch was expanded. By the end of the decade, all of the present huts were in place except for Mizpah Spring, which was built in 1964, and the roadside hostel at Crawford Notch. Others were improved, expanded, or replaced, but the system was essentially complete.

Today the system consists of eight trailside huts plus Joe Dodge Lodge at Pinkham Notch Visitor Center and the Crawford Notch Hostel. The huts reach from Lonesome Lake, west of Franconia Notch, to Carter Notch, east of Pinkham. They are connected by the Appalachian Trail and other trails maintained by the AMC and the Forest Service. They are operated as a nonprofit service to the hiking public, offering "mountain hospitality for all."

Each of the huts has a resident crew of young men and women who pack in much of the food and other needed supplies. Hearty meals are available at each hut. Bunks and blankets are provided so that the hut-hopper need not carry a sleeping bag (except in winter, as detailed later). All huts are open from early June to mid-September; several are open from mid-May until mid-October; and currently three are open year-round: Zealand Falls, Crawford Notch, and Carter Notch. Pinkham Notch Visitor Center is also open all year. Since the dates of operation vary somewhat from year to year, the prospective hut user should obtain specific information from either Pinkham Notch Visitor Center, P.O. Box 298, Gorham, NH 03581, 603-466-2727; or the AMC office in Boston, 5 Joy Street, Boston, MA 02108; 617-523-0636.

All of the huts serve breakfast and dinner family-style at fixed times: breakfast at seven, dinner at six. A modest assortment of trail food is available for purchase—raisins, chocolate bars, and, usually, fresh fruit. Although full lunches are not prepared, hot soup and hot and cold drinks are usually available. Hikers should carry some food for emergencies; it is a good idea always to have a modest amount of food in one's pack.

Reservations are required and can be made through the reservations desk at Pinkham Notch by mail or telephone. It is best to call directly (603-466-2727), for some of the huts may be fully booked well in advance, especially on Saturday and holiday nights. Walk-ins are accommodated if space is available and will always be taken care of if the hour is late and the weather is bad. But hut crews need to know in advance how many guests to cook for. *The Guide to AMC Huts and Lodges,* with reservation information, dates of opening and closing, and type of service available at each hut, can be obtained by writing to

Pinkham Notch Visitor Center. Members of the AMC are entitled to a discount. (Information on membership can be obtained at the huts or from the AMC office in Boston.)

Sleeping accommodations vary from hut to hut. Some have two large bunkrooms with individual tiered bunks. Others have several small bunkrooms, each accommodating from 4 to 12 persons. Each bunk has three wool blankets and a pillow. (The crew members have very imaginative ways of demonstrating correct blanket-folding technique.) Hikers should bring a sheet sleeping sack and pillow cover. When possible, hutmasters keep families and hiking groups together. In order to use the space most efficiently, bunkrooms are not kept rigidly segregated by sex. This follows a European tradition in which the *Matratzenlager*—a sleeping loft with mattresses laid side by side across the width of the room—is occupied by men and women indiscriminately.

Each hut also keeps a log for visitors to sign, and it provides some of the most interesting reading one is likely to encounter in the huts.

Each of the huts has its own—usually unique—water supply and sewage-disposal systems. Most of the huts are supplied with water from nearby springs. Some are supplied with lake water. Whatever the source, state health regulations require treatment to ensure potability. The water is chlorinated and tested regularly. Flow from some of the springs fluctuates and becomes rather low during dry years. Water should be used sparingly.

Where soils are thin and the bedrock is near the surface, sewage treatment and disposal is a problem. Because of local conditions, each hut must deal with this in a unique way. At some, where the water supply is limited, human waste is collected in 55-gallon drums and hauled out by helicopter. At others, standard septic-tank systems have been installed.

Because waste disposal is such a problem at the huts, some of what is packed in must also be packed out—bottles, cans, even cardboard cartons. So please take all of your trash out with you.

All but two of the huts are accessible only by trail. In the early days, all of the supplies, from blankets to baking powder, were carried to the huts on strong backs. There was great rivalry among the hutmen over who could carry the heaviest load. Records were set and broken with great regularity. Each of the huts has a record sheet listing the names of Old Hutmen who had been distinguished with incredible feats of load-carrying. This was great for the ego but hard on the knees. Today much of the heaviest stuff is airlifted in by helicopter before the beginning of the summer season. Each hut has its own landing platform or delivery area, but it is unlikely that you will ever see it used. During the summer, the helicopter is used only for emergencies and for such tasks as hauling out sewage barrels that can be done in no other way.

There has been some controversy over the appropriateness of helicopters in the wilderness. But a few minutes' conversation with an Old Hutman who is still bothered with damaged knees might silence at least some of the controversy. Hut crews still get plenty of exercise, for they regularly pack in fresh supplies on their backs. But today, pack loads for both sexes are limited to about 80 pounds.

Packing is part of the mystique of being a member of a hut crew (or "croo," as they prefer to spell it—more correctly, "Da Croo"). Suggestions that load packing be sup-

Crew members pack supplies to the huts daily. Paul Mozell.

planted by helicopter delivery of all supplies are universally derided by the crew members, male and female alike. They see packing as a part of the total operation of the hut, and they want to "do it all." Another reason, perhaps, is that packing, at least with moderate loads, is a great way to attain and maintain a prime physical condition.

For one of the high huts, supplies must be packed *down* the trail. Supplies for Lakes of the Clouds Hut are trucked up the Mt. Washington Auto Road, then packed down to the hut. Veteran members of the crew will admit that this is considered to be the worst packing of all. Packing a heavy load down the Crawford Path is murderous on knees.

Although the huts were built and are operated by the AMC, all but one are on state or federal land. The one exception is Madison Spring Hut, built on an acre of land donated to the AMC by Brown's Lumber Company before the White Mountain National Forest was established. Lonesome Lake Hut is on state land; the buildings were constructed by the state of New Hampshire and are leased to the AMC for operation as a hut. All of the others operate with special use permits from the U.S. Forest Service. The huts are considered by the Forest Service to be performing a public service. As such, they are open to everyone on a nondiscriminatory basis. AMC members are given no special priority in reservations and no special treatment at the huts. Members do receive a small discount on the overnight rate, however, in recognition of the fact that the huts were built with funds and labor donated by AMC members.

The huts are more than mountain inns. They serve as important emergency communication links in the mountains. Each of the huts has a two-way radio that provides communication with Pinkham Notch. A weather forecast is transmitted to each hut at 8 A.M. and posted for the convenience and safety of hikers. The huts also serve as operations centers for the all-too-frequent search and rescue operations. Although the New Hampshire Fish and Game Department is charged with the responsibility "to conduct search and rescue operations in woodlands and inland waters" in the White Mountains, many of the mountain rescues are effected by the hut crews. It is a volunteer effort that is carried out with a great sense of responsibility by the young men and women who run the huts. A brief account of a minor incident that could have been major will illustrate:

> I was walking down to the Lakes of the Clouds Hut from the summit of Mt. Washington one blustery June day with my young son and his friend when we met a man with an injured leg. He was accompanying two women and two

toddlers; they were planning to spend the night at the hut. He had slipped and fallen, gashing his knee and twisting an ankle rather badly. Fortunately, a hiker with first-aid equipment had bandaged the knee properly. But the man was having some difficulty walking, and it was not at all clear that he could walk to the hut. Furthermore, the two women with the young children were quite apprehensive, for the toddlers were making slow progress on the rocks of the Crawford Path. It was mid-afternoon and, quite typically, it started to rain. I sent the boys ahead to the hut with the message that if we did not arrive by 5:30 P.M., someone should come looking for us for it probably meant that we were having difficulty. I walked with the group as they made their slow and, for the man, painful way down. We arrived at the hut tired and wet a few minutes after the appointed hour, just in time to stop three of the crew from heading up the trail with emergency equipment. Even though the hut was full and the crew was preparing dinner for 90 people, they were prepared to conduct a rescue mission. After dinner, one of the crew (they all have first-aid training) washed and bandaged the cut, and all was well.

We can all be thankful that the hut crews are there, ready, willing, and able to carry out a mountain rescue should the need arise.

The huts serve other useful functions as well. Each summer, volunteer scientists exchange their expertise for a short period of lodging at one of the huts. These "hut naturalists" conduct after-dinner walks for those who may be interested in the natural history of the hut environs. They also give informal instruction to the members of the hut crews who may then conduct their own informal nature walks. The huts serve as a base for mountain leadership courses in which camp counselors and leaders learn how to take their youth groups on safe mountain trips.

Indeed, this educational function is considered by the AMC to be the main purpose of the Club: "to encourage public respect for the natural environment through providing opportunities for the enjoyment of its beauty and the wise stewardship of its use." Nowhere is this commitment more evident than in the huts. Every attempt is made to operate the huts in an environmentally sensitive and ecologically appropriate manner. Hut crews and hut naturalists, in their after-dinner nature walks, are likely to stress the problems of maintaining the quality of the natural environment in the face of ever-increasing use. One person pounding the tundra in the vicinity of a hut may not seem to make much difference. But a hundred or a thousand "waffle-stompers" can kill fragile vegetation, leaving unsightly bare patches. Most of the huts have a self-guided nature walk that will lead the hut visitor to interesting features in the immediate environs. Information on these walks is contained in subsequent chapters.

Nevertheless, the above-timberline huts provide a base for exploring the fascinating land of the alpine tundra. The weather above timberline is so severe that few tents can withstand the high winds that occur even in the summertime. And the tundra, seemingly so rugged in this violent climate, is also very fragile. The place where a tent was pitched on the tundra 10 years ago can still be identified. The tundra is attuned to some kinds of insults, but not others. It recovers very slowly. To protect this unique resource, the Forest Service prohibits camping above timberline in summer. In winter, camping is permitted only where there is two feet or more of snow, but not on frozen bodies of water.

The rest of this book tells something about the natural history of the area that is served by the huts. Information on the weather and climate of the White Mountains is given extensive treatment because of its importance in contributing to the comfort and safety of the mountain hiker. Brief chapters give an overview of the geological setting and the plant ecology of the area. These are not intended to be complete. A list of useful guidebooks is given in the appendix.

Subsequent chapters provide information on each of the huts: how to get there, how to get to adjacent huts, day-hikes in each area. Although the information is primarily for summer visitors, some information is provided for the visitor to the winter huts (Carter Notch and Zealand Falls) and Pinkham Notch Visitor Center.

Although this book is all that is really needed to give you an idea of what to do and see at each hut, do not rely solely on it for trail routes. Be sure to have a good set of maps and a compass with you. This book will also have failed if it doesn't lead you to explore other sources of information. Each of the huts has a collection of information specific to that hut as well as a small library of guidebooks. And the hut crews are perhaps the best resource. They can provide you with much information on the local flora and fauna, trail conditions, weather, and whatever else you would like to know about things to do and see within a day's walk of the hut.

Many people make a distinction between the "high huts" (Greenleaf, Lakes of the Clouds, and Madison) and all the rest. I have ignored this distinction except in one place—the next chapter on the weather and climate of the White Mountains. The high huts are all above timberline. Their weather and climate are much different from that of the lower, below-timberline huts. Data from the summit of Mt. Washington have been used to characterize the above-timberline weather. Data from Pinkham Notch are more appropriate to the below-timberline huts.

1
White Mountain Weather and Climate

THE huts span an elevational range of 3,000 feet, from 2,000 feet at Pinkham Notch Visitor Center to just over 5,000 feet at Lakes of the Clouds. Normally this elevation difference would not signify a very great change in climate—perhaps 10° difference in temperature, a little more precipitation at the higher hut, perhaps a little more wind—but there is more than just an elevation change at work here. Lakes of the Clouds Hut is above timberline and exposed to the full fury of the jet-stream winds that frequently funnel across the Presidentials. Pinkham Notch, on the lee side of the range and in a deep wooded valley, is sheltered from the worst of the winds. In bioclimatic terms—that is, in terms of human exposure—the difference in winter will be from a merely cold and snowy climate at Pinkham to a bitterly and dangerously cold climate above timberline, one in which exposed flesh will freeze in a matter of minutes.

Even in summer the difference in climate between the valleys and the exposed summits can be dramatic, as almost any hiker who has climbed Mt. Washington in shorts and a light shirt can testify. Daytime temperatures in the 70s in the valley may make such light apparel appropriate. But with an afternoon temperature in the low 50s on the summit, a 25-mile-an-hour wind blowing, and the sun obscured by an enveloping cloud, windchill will produce

Weather in winter can vary from cold and snowy in the valleys to dangerously cold and windy on the summits. Being prepared is essential. These hikers are climbing Mt. Madison. Paul Mozell.

conditions that in terms of human physiology and comfort are well below freezing.

The climate of the White Mountains is a patterned mosaic, patterned in space and time by the interaction of the great currents of air that swirl across the Appalachians with a complicated array of slopes, peaks, ridges, and valleys. During periods of atmospheric quiescence, when skies are clear and winds are light, the climate differentiates into an infinite variety of patterns, with each little topographic niche having its own special microclimate. At other times, when storm clouds scud across the ridges and the skies are filled with slanting streaks of rain, the weather is nearly the same everywhere.

A hiker visiting the entire string of huts will almost certainly encounter the entire range of seasonal weather that the White Mountains have to offer. The route takes one from valley bottoms at 1,500 feet elevation to the summit of Mt. Washington at 6,288 feet; from the mixed hardwoods of the lower elevations, through the spruce-fir forests and timberline krummholz to the Arctic tundra that clings precariously to the highest ridges and peaks. Weather systems follow one another with startling speed.

Major Climatic Controls

The White Mountains lie in the zone of the westerlies. High in the atmosphere, the air swirls around the North Temperate Zone in great undulations, vast sinuous curves that move now toward the southeast, now curling around to the northeast, then swinging around again to a flow to the southeast. There are usually four to six of these sinusoidal curves to the circulation pattern of the northern hemisphere. The width of the United States is just about enough to hold one wave; when one crest or ridge lies along the Pacific coast, another crest usually occupies the eastern seaboard. In between, the air above courses southeastward through the Rockies, curves northeastward through the Great Plains, and turns east along the north Atlantic shore. On its way through the southern plains, the air picks up moisture streaming north from the Gulf of Mexico and brings it to the Great Lakes region. Storms developing in the air move down the St. Lawrence Valley and bring rain and snow to the upper Midwest and New England. Temperatures remain mild, however, as warmer air from the south mixes in.

When the sinusoidal pattern is displaced eastward, the crest is centered over the Rocky Mountains, and the trough occupies a position along the Appalachians. Cold air from Canada then sweeps across the Great Lakes and the mountains of the Northeast. When this cold air comes into contact with warmer and moister air from the Gulf of Mexico and the south Atlantic, storms tend to develop off the coast and move northeastward. If they are steered close to the shoreline, air spiraling counterclockwise around the storm center brings northeasterly winds to New England—the classic "northeaster." In the winter, the air has a long trajectory over cold northern waters and arrives over land ready to condense its moisture into snow. As the air rises over the mountains, it drops the moisture, and a heavy New England snowfall results.

As sometimes happens, coastal storms may move in a more easterly direction. The mid-Atlantic states and the southern coast of New England will then receive the bulk of the precipitation, while northern New England remains in drier air.

When the typical sinusoidal pattern is absent, a strong west-to-east air flow dominates. The jet stream is displaced northward into Canada. Air arriving over New England has come from the region off the Pacific coast in the Gulf of Alaska. After passing over the western mountains, it is relatively warm and dry. Storms developing in this airstream move rapidly eastward and are not heavy rain producers for they do not have access to the supply of moisture in the Gulf of Mexico.

Two semipermanent pressure systems in the Atlantic Ocean greatly affect the flow of air into the Northeast and the direction that storms take in their passage through the region. In the south Atlantic, a huge mound of air circulating clockwise stretches from the southeast coast nearly to the shores of Europe and North Africa. In its eastern portion, this is known as the Azores High; its western extension is called the Bermuda High. In the summer, the western edge of the Bermuda High pushes inland over the southeastern states and funnels warm, moist air northeastward.

In the north Atlantic, off the southern coasts of Greenland and Iceland, lies another great pressure center: the Icelandic Low. Swirling counterclockwise around its center, the winds act as a great suction to draw in the storms that head northeastward off the east coast of North America. When the Icelandic Low is displaced southwestward toward the Atlantic provinces, it intensifies these storms just off the coast. New England and the neighboring Canadian provinces may then be in for a prolonged period of storms and cold northerly winds.

It was a storm of this sort that brought the heaviest 24-hour snowfall on record to the White Mountains. On November 22, 1943, a coastal storm stalled just off the southern New England coast. For 24 hours it funneled moist air over the land and up the slopes of the mountains. Before it was over, Pinkham Notch had recorded 51 inches of new snow, Berlin recorded 55 inches, and Randolph, 56 inches. The heaviest amounts fell on the northern slopes; in the southern "shadow," amounts reached only 20 inches.

The Icelandic Low and the Bermuda High conspire to ensure that most of the upper-level air flow across northern New England is from the west. Only during transient storms does the wind blow from other quadrants. This strong westerly flow interacts with the mountain topography to produce one of the extraordinary characteristics of White Mountain weather: the extremely high wind speeds above timberline and especially on Mt. Washington. Strong currents of air from the west and northwest accelerate as they squeeze over the Presidential Range. The result is an average annual wind speed of 35 miles per hour at the summit observatory.

Typically, wind speeds exceed 90 mph during every month of the year. Hurricane-force winds (greater than 75 mph) occur on half of all winter days and on two to four days in summer months. Combined with low year-round temperatures, the winds produce conditions that are comparable with those found in the Antarctic.

Another way to look at the wind is to ask, What is the probability that the wind will exceed a specified velocity at a particular time during the year? Figure 1 on page 7 is based on long-term observation of wind speed at the summit of Mt. Washington and answers this question. For example, in June, there is a probability of about 75 percent that the wind speed will be greater than 20 mph at any time. The probability is 10 percent that the wind speed will be greater than 40 mph. In January, the windiest month, the probability is 60 percent that at any time the wind will be blowing faster than 40 mph.

Outdoor Bioclimate

The hiker or skier exposed to the elements reacts to meteorological factors that control the flow of heat to or from the body. In summer, high air temperatures, high humidity, lots of sunshine, and little wind may conspire to make the hiker uncomfortably warm if not dangerously hot. In winter, the same weather factors may work adversely: low temperature, high relative humidity, cloudy skies, and high wind will carry body heat away so fast as to produce dangerously cold conditions.

What is needed is a way of integrating temperature, wind, and humidity into a single index that indicates their

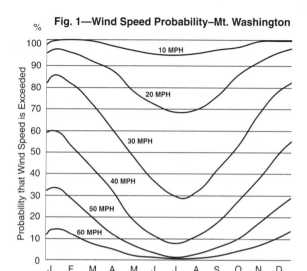

Fig. 1—Wind Speed Probability–Mt. Washington

(y-axis: Probability that Wind Speed is Exceeded, %; x-axis: J F M A M J J A S O N D)

Curves labeled: 10 MPH, 20 MPH, 30 MPH, 40 MPH, 50 MPH, 60 MPH

Source: Widger, W.K., Jr., and A.R. Mignone Jr., 1977, "Theoretical Wind Power for Mount Washington. " *Mount Washington Observatory News Bulletin,* 18(3):50-57

This chart shows the chances for each month (along the bottom) that wind will exceed a given speed at the summit of Mt. Washington. For example, in June, there is a probability of about 75 percent that the wind will exceed 20 mph at any given time.

combined effect on human comfort. When temperatures are low, high winds increase heat loss from the body, making the air feel colder than it actually is. A windchill temperature can be devised that tells how much colder the air feels when the wind is blowing than when the wind is light. The other major factor that affects human comfort, especially when temperatures are high, is atmospheric humidity. Any combination of windchill temperature and a measure of humidity can be interpreted in terms of human comfort. We can use average monthly conditions to calculate an index that will then indicate the average bioclimate of that month.

The diagram used to plot such values is shown in Figure 2 (on page 9). It uses monthly precipitation instead of humidity, which is not observed at most rural and mountain observation stations. In exposed locations, average monthly wind speed is used to calculate the windchill temperature. In protected locations, such as beneath forest canopies, wind speeds are low and air temperature and windchill temperature are equal. Comfort sensations are indicated as zones on the diagram. When points representing average conditions for each month are plotted (starting with "1" for January) and joined by lines, a curve or "climogram" showing annual progression of outdoor bioclimate is obtained.

At low windchill temperatures, the various zones can be interpreted in terms of the clothing that should be worn and the precautions that should be taken by those venturing into the backcountry. Zone I: comfortable with normal precautions. Zone II: work and travel become uncomfortable unless properly clothed. Zone III: work and travel become hazardous unless properly clothed. Heavy outer clothing is necessary. Zone IV: unprotected skin will freeze with direct exposure over prolonged period. Heavy outer clothing is mandatory. Zone V: unprotected skin can freeze in one minute with direct exposure. Multiple layers of clothing are mandatory. Adequate face protection becomes important. Work and travel alone are not advisable.

The climogram for Pinkham Notch is representative of low elevation areas in the forest where wind speeds are low. The climogram for the summit of Mt. Washington is representative of above-timberline areas. It should be remembered that the plotted points represent average conditions and therefore characterize the climate of the area.

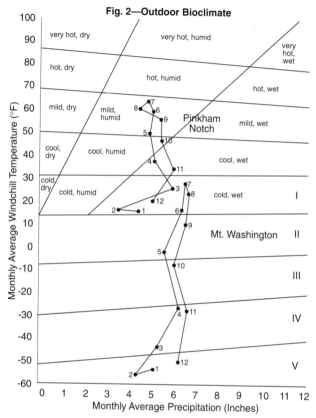

Fig. 2—Outdoor Bioclimate

Comparing windchill temperature to precipitation, this chart calculates how comfortable you can expect to be during a given month (numbers 1-12). Numbers I-V are zones of comfort and are explained in the text. For example, Pinkham in May is classed as "mild/humid," while the summit in May is Zone II, and can be uncomfortable unless properly clothed. The chart also compares Pinkham Notch to the summit of Mt. Washington. For example, conditions in January, February, March, and December at Pinkham are comparable to June, July, and August at the summit.

The weather at any particular time probably will be different from the average, better or worse.

In the months from late spring to early fall, the bioclimate of Pinkham Notch is classed as mild/humid. April and October border on the cool/humid to cool/wet. The winter months from January through March are cold/wet. On the summit of Mt. Washington, the summer bioclimate is similar to Pinkham's winter climate in terms of human comfort; that is, similar kinds of clothing would have to be worn to provide the same degree of comfort and protection. In the fall, the climate of the summit deteriorates rapidly, going from very cold in September to bitterly cold in October, dangerously cold in November, to worse in the winter months. Indeed, bioclimatically speaking, there is no summer on the summit.

With this as background, we can now take a more detailed look at the progression of climate through the seasons.

Summer

For the hut user, the beginning of summer might well be defined as the date the huts open for full operation, normally in early June. This time also makes bioclimatic sense. By early June, the outdoor bioclimate below timberline is well into the mild/humid zone where it remains through September. Summer circulation patterns begin to take hold in June. Storms moving across Canada from the west stay north of the mountains, often bringing light rain and no well-defined fronts. Storms from the lower Midwest still follow down the St. Lawrence Valley, but these are less intense than winter storms following the same track. As the sun approaches the summer solstice, the summer pattern becomes firmly entrenched. Air mass weather predominates. Skies fill with puffy cumulus clouds, some of which build to giant thunderheads. Although May averages only one thunderstorm, by June the number rises to four.

By early June the average daily temperature has reached 50°F. Daytime maximum temperatures are about 65°F; nighttime minimums are in the low 40s. The temperature will fall below 41°F on only five nights; half the time it will be above 48°F. Daytime highs will be above 80°F on five days and above 70°F on 15. Frosts are rare except in open places subject to air drainage.

June is a wet month in the mountains. Rain in excess of 0.1 inch can be expected on about 10 days, while more than half have some kind of precipitation. Most of the rain comes in showers, although passing storms may bring one or two periods of steadier rain. About three days will have heavy rainfalls in excess of 0.5 inch.

Above timberline, winter has not yet completely relinquished its grip. At least one snowfall can be expected, although the amount is usually only an inch or so and it melts quickly. However, as much as eight inches have fallen in June. Most of the snow comes as the aftermath of a cyclonic storm that is followed by a cold, unstable air mass from the northwest. Such storms usually bring rain, which may change to snow briefly when the associated cold front passes. Rain occurs frequently.

Temperatures remain on the cool side, with afternoon readings generally in the 50s, rarely reaching 60°F. Winds average 27 mph at the summit of Mt. Washington but can be expected to reach hurricane force on four days in June. More than two-thirds of the days are overcast; the summit and much of the area above timberline will often be in the clouds with reduced visibility.

The typical June day above timberline is raw and windy, with the summits and ridges in and out of the clouds, and usually with some rain.

July is the warmest summer month. Typically, a weak low-pressure area in eastern Canada and a high-pressure area along the southeastern coast work together to funnel hot, moist air from the Gulf of Mexico into New England. Hot, humid weather prevails even in the mountains. Such conditions may prevail for days before giving way to a more westerly or northwesterly flow, bringing drier air from the far west or central Canada.

Daytime highs reach into the 70s; the afternoon maximum will be above 75°F nearly half the time. Nevertheless, oppressively hot weather is rare, and temperatures above 85°F can be expected on only one day. Nights are generally cool, with minimum temperatures below 55°F half the time. The temperature fails to go below 60°F only 10 percent of the time—about three days.

Above timberline, temperatures are markedly lower. On the summit of Mt. Washington, maximum temperatures may be expected to be above 60°F 25 percent of the time—about eight days. At the other end of the scale, maximum temperatures can be expected to remain below 52°F on another eight days. Cloudiness remains about the same as June—about half the days are predominantly overcast. About two-thirds of the days are cloudy, with the highest summits actually in the clouds. Clear days are rather rare: about four days in the low country, two above timberline. Fog is rare at low elevations, about two days.

Precipitation can be expected on about half the days in July. About five of these days will have thunderstorms. Some may be severe, with hail and gusty winds. Occasional cold fronts bring snow flurries above timberline, but rarely any accumulation.

Days shorten perceptibly in August. By midmonth, day length is down to 13 hours from the maximum of 15 hours at the summer solstice. But the Earth and atmosphere are thermally sluggish and cool down slowly. August temperatures are only slightly cooler than July temperatures. Storm tracks are displaced far to the north, and low pressure disturbances course from west to east across Canada. Sometimes the fronts from these systems affect White Mountain weather, but usually only with cloudiness or light rain.

By August, the atmosphere is beginning to dry out somewhat. Thunderstorms are less frequent, down to about three. Cloudy weather reaches its lowest frequency; only about one-third of the days are overcast, and there are an average of six clear days.

Although average temperatures decrease slightly during August, the combination of drier air and clearer skies leads to the highest temperatures recorded in the region. It was in this month in 1975 that the temperature at the summit of Mt. Washington reached a sweltering 72°F! I have personally experienced a 70°F temperature at the summit in August, a memorable experience. But don't count on it. Three-fourths of the time, the maximum will be below 60°F. At lower elevations, however, temperatures are more moderate. Daytime highs can be expected to be above 72°F half the time, and will be below 45°F on about four days, most likely toward the end of the month.

Except for fewer thunderstorms, precipitation frequently remains about the same as in July. Fog is rare at low elevations but remains often—about 75 percent of the time—on the ridges and peaks above timberline.

Autumn

The autumn months of September and October are without doubt the most delightful months of the year. Storm tracks remain far to the north in September, but as the sun approaches the equator, its hold on summer diminishes. Drier tropical air funnels northward, and the number of clear days increases. Indeed, the highest frequency of clear days occurs in September and October: about seven or eight per month. Even above timberline, five or six clear days may be expected in each month.

Frosts become more common toward the end of the month, and by October nearly half the days will see temperatures drop below the freezing mark. Also by October, daytime highs are decreasing; only about four days will have temperatures above 70°F. This month usually has the first snowfall of consequence. Normally the ground will be covered with a few inches by the end of October. Occasionally, however, much heavier snows will occur in the fall; the record for Pinkham Notch in October is 30 inches.

Above timberline, winter has set in. By October, the daytime maximum temperatures will be below 40°F most of the time, and the lows will be below freezing on 75 percent of the days. Average snowfall is greater than 12 inches. Wind speed is also up, averaging 34 mph on the summit.

But October usually brings a spell of Indian summer. A stagnating high-pressure area over the mid-Atlantic states means clear skies and sluggish air movement. Although the sun is past the equinox, it still has enough energy to produce a period of warm days when the temperature remains above freezing even at night. At the summit of Mt. Washington, an average of eight days are clear.

Some of these will be Indian summer days, others will be caused by a flood of clear, cool Canadian air.

Winter

November brings winter to the White Mountains. The mean temperature drops to just above the freezing mark at Pinkham and to 21°F at the summit of Mt. Washington. Storm tracks begin to move into their typical winter pattern. The trans-Canada track moves southward from Hudson Bay so that storms originating in Alberta frequently move eastward just north of New England. Coastal storms also increase in intensity as cold air from the north flows over the Gulf Stream and triggers their formation. These storms bring snow as often as they bring rain. By the end of November, the snowpack is normally about a foot deep, although there have been years when it was three or four feet deep. Occasionally, when the major November storm track is down the St. Lawrence Valley, little snow will fall.

Daytime maximum temperatures are generally in the low 40s, while nighttime lows are in the 20s. Cloudiness increases slightly from the previous month, decreasing the number of clear days from eight to five.

Above timberline, winter is in full swing. Clouds cover the summits on three-quarters of the days. Only three November days are classed as clear. Much of the precipitation comes as snow, although the inland-tracking storms may bring enough warm, moist air on southerly winds to keep rain coming down even on the summit. The average November snowfall is 30 inches, with actual amounts ranging from 6 inches (in 1953) to 87 inches (in 1968). Wind increases also, averaging 39 mph.

December 21 marks the winter solstice—the day having the shortest period between sunrise and sunset. In the White Mountains, this day is only 8 hours and 30 minutes long. Winter storms course northeastward along the Atlantic coastline, usually bringing snow to the high country, but sometimes bringing rain to lower elevations. By the end of the month, the snowpack at Pinkham Notch normally reaches a depth of about two feet; the least amount of December snowfall recorded in 22 years was 13 inches.

The deep winter months of December, January, and February are quite similar in their climatic patterns. The main difference is in the depth of snowpack, which normally reaches a maximum in March. At Pinkham, the increase is from two feet in December to four feet in March. There is usually at least a foot of snow on the ground by the end of January.

Skies remain predominantly cloudy throughout the winter; half the days are overcast and only five or six are clear. Precipitation also occurs on half the days, most of it in the form of snow.

Above timberline, arctic conditions prevail throughout the winter. Precipitation occurs on nearly two-thirds of the days and most of this is in the form of snow: about 40 inches each month. Winds reach their highest average speeds, greater than 40 mph from December through March. On half of all winter days, winds will reach hurricane force, 75 mph or more. On those days, windchill temperatures will plummet to 60° or 70° below zero, an extremely dangerous level.

By the end of March, the spring equinox has passed, and the sun is above the horizon longer than it is below. Nevertheless, winter storm tracks still prevail; clashes between the increasingly moist air from the south and the still-frigid air from the north bring some of winter's heaviest storms. The blizzard of 1888 started on March 11 and dumped more than four feet of snow in central Connecticut with lesser amounts in northern New England.

But rain is as likely as snow in March, especially at lower elevations. The greatest floods in New England's history occurred in March 1936, when extremely heavy rains fell on a deep snowpack. Pinkham Notch received 11 inches in two days; before the month was over, 24 inches of rain had fallen.

Although temperatures have started their slow climb to summertime levels, the average March temperature at Pinkham is still well below freezing—25°F. The daily maximum averages 37°F, and on only four days will the maximum reach 50°F. Minimums are in the upper teens and will go below zero on a couple of nights.

Above timberline, deep winter remains through April. The average daily maximum temperature is only 29°F at the summit of Mt. Washington during this month. And the maximum will be above freezing on only about a third of the days. Snowfall remains high during April. Indeed, each month from November through April averages between 24 and 27 inches at the summit. Skies remain predominantly cloudy and foggy, and nearly two-thirds of April days have some kind of precipitation. About four days are clear.

Although the snowpack has started to diminish in April, the average at lower elevations is still better than two feet. Ski touring is usually possible early in the month, but becomes questionable by the end.

Spring

The warm sunshine of May hastens the melting of the winter snowpack. Although a considerable amount of snow usually covers the ground at the beginning of the month, little remains by the end, except in a rare year. A major exception is in the glacial cirque of Tuckerman Ravine, which often has skiable snow until the end of June. The two or three snowfalls that usually occur during May do little to add to the snowpack.

As the snow disappears, the land rapidly becomes warmer than the large water bodies nearby, the Great Lakes and the Atlantic Ocean. High pressure starts to develop over the Great Lakes, forcing storm tracks northward into Ontario. The Bermuda High extends westward and inhibits storm development in the Gulf of Mexico, where the major winter storms come from. The result is a decrease in the number and intensity of cyclonic storms affecting the White Mountains and an increase in the number of air-mass showers. An occasional shower will develop into a thunderstorm in May.

Temperatures climb rapidly, with the average daytime maximum near 60°F and the minimum near 40°F. On nearly a third of the days, afternoon temperatures will climb to 68°F or above. Precipitation amounts remain near the year-round monthly average of five inches.

Above timberline, the climate has started to improve slightly. The mean temperature is up to 34°F. The daily maximum average is 41°F and can be expected to reach 50°F on seven days. However, minimums still go below freezing two-thirds of the time. Wind speeds decrease slightly, averaging 30 mph at the summit. As a result, the bioclimate is still in the "very cold" zone. Protection from winter weather is still required.

The hut user must be prepared for a wide variety of climates, depending on the season and the location of the huts to be visited. A brief summary is given here of the conditions that should be expected and prepared for during the time of the year that each hut is currently open. The minimum weather protection that should be carried is also suggested. From mid-June to mid-September, good protection against rain and wind is essential above timberline. A waterproof parka and rain pants, or a cagoule, provide better protection from the wind than does a poncho. Trousers should be worn or carried. A warm wool sweater or a down or fiberfill vest or shirt, a wool hat, and wool mittens or gloves are *mandatory*. Sturdy, ankle-high hiking boots should be worn.

Below timberline, a poncho can usually be relied on for adequate rain protection. A warm sweater is necessary and full-length trousers are desirable to protect against cold rain. Hat and gloves are desirable.

In the month before or just after the normal hut season, the hut hiker must be prepared for the possibility of a late-spring or early-fall snow shower. Equipment appropriate to above-timberline travel in midsummer is necessary.

For trips to the winter huts, full protection against winter storms is necessary. Wool pants, long underwear, several sweaters or a down or fiberfill vest, a winter parka, wool mittens and shells, and a wool hat are absolutely necessary. Sturdy, insulated boots should be worn. Most cross-country boots are too thin for adequate protection against winter cold on a long, cold-weather ski tour. A good winter sleeping bag is also required for use at the hut. It is also good insurance against the possibility that the tourer might have to spend a night in the open due to a mishap.

2
Geology

▼

THE geological story of the White Mountains begins some 500 million years ago when a vast ocean separated the North American continent from a giant land mass to the east. At that time the continental shoreline was about 200 to 300 miles west of its present location. The continental shelf stretched eastward to somewhere near the present Vermont–New Hampshire boundary before it dropped off into the oceanic deeps.

Streams and rivers running eastward toward the sea from the mountains along the continental margin carried sediments that spread out along the continental shelf. For many millions of years, the fast-running and turbulent streams carried their suspended loads of sand, silt, and mud out into the proto–Atlantic Ocean, depositing layer upon layer of sediments. In addition, active volcanoes contributed ash and lava to the ocean floor. As the sediments accumulated, they sank of their own weight. The huge pressures so generated gradually transformed them into sandstone and slate, forming the precursor of what are now known as the Albee formation and the Ammonoosuc volcanics.

Subsequently, unknown forces started the two continents bordering the proto-Atlantic to move inexorably toward each other. As the continents moved, the giant rock plate forming the ocean floor was forced under the continental margin. The sedimentary rocks that formed the continental shelf were pushed up and buckled to form a chain of high mountains. Where the rock plate beneath the ocean turned down to slide under the continent, weak spots developed and a chain of volcanoes formed an arc of islands off the coast. These too moved westward toward the shore of the North American continent. This period of mountain building, the so-called Taconic orogeny, took place some 460 million years ago, in the middle Ordovician period. At the time, the continental margin was still west of its present location, the result of the uplifting of the ocean sediments.

For many millions of years, erosion took its toll in the uplifted mountains. Sediments again washed their way eastward into the narrowing ocean, carried down by the workings of the streams and rivers that coursed their slopes. Thick layers of mud were laid down seaward of the continental margin. Pressure gradually squeezed and transformed these sediments into layers of sandstone and shale and eventually into a black-and-white banded gneiss now known as the lower member of the Littleton formation. The dark layers are chiefly black and white mica with some quartz and feldspar. The lighter layers that look like granite are made up chiefly of quartz and feldspar.

On top of this was deposited a rather thin layer of impure limestone. This was later changed into a hard, compact rock composed of dark and greenish grains of diopside and needles of actinolite. More sediments were piled on top, to complete the deposition of the Littleton formation. The upper member, composed originally of sand and mud, changed with time into interbedded quartzite and mica schist. The schist contains various minerals: sillimanite, staurolite, garnet, black tourmaline, and, of course, mica. The composition of the schist varies from place to place.

The filling of the sandwich, the thin (0–200 feet) layer of impure limestone, is one of the characteristic features of bedrock in the Presidential Range. It is exposed in numerous places and, because of its uniformity and characteristic appearance, has been of great help in solving the puzzle of White Mountain geology. This layer is the Boott member of the Littleton formation and is visible in a good many places in the Presidentials. Some of the best of these are described in subsequent chapters.

In addition to the erosion, the mountains themselves sank into the ocean. Eventually, the eastern New England area was again underwater. It remained that way for a long time, as the Eurasian continent ground its slow way westward.

Eventually the two continents joined to form one continuous continent (called Pangea) about 375 million years ago, in middle Devonian time. The mountains of New England again rose and the proto–Atlantic Ocean was no more. Indeed, one could have walked along the chain to the mountains of Scandinavia, with which they were continuous. This was a time of intense folding and faulting. The sediments to the west of the main chain were crumpled into the series of long ridges so evident today in the Blue Ridge Mountains of the central Appalachians. This period of mountain building, the so-called Acadian orogeny, lifted eastern New England above sea level for the first time.

Rocks again became plastic under intense heat and pressure. They yielded to the squeezing and pulling and folded like taffy in a taffy-pull. Until this time the sediments of the Littleton formation were still recognizable as sediments although pressure had transformed them into shales and sandstones. But now the heat and pressure generated by the compressive forces that produced the folding also initiated the metamorphosis of the sedimentary rocks into forms no longer recognizable as sediments. The sedimentary rocks were generally modified to gneiss, quartzite, and schist, whereas the volcanic rocks recrystallized to form granite. Kinsman quartz monzonite, exposed between Kinsman Notch and Lonesome Lake, is an example of granite formed by the intense heat and pressure generated by the continental collision. Folded rocks can be seen many places in the mountains, especially in the Presidential Range—on the southeast side of Mt. John Quincy Adams, for example. The massif of Mt. Washington itself was formed from a giant fold in the Littleton formation (see geologic cross section along the Appalachian Trail, pages 26–27). At the time, however, "Mt. Washington" was still buried deep beneath the surface. The upper part of the Littleton formation, now exposed as the summit, was transformed into compact quartzites and schists that are among the most wear-resistant rocks in New England.

But as the continents joined to form Pangea, so they ultimately split apart, drifting slowly to their present positions. Indeed, the drift is going on today. The split, which started 200 million years ago in the Jurassic period, started east of the point where they had originally joined. Volcanoes developed along tension zones as the continents drifted apart, but these were short-lived. Some faulting occurred, notably along the Ammonoosuc fault, which runs from Fabyan to Randolph. And the so-called White Mountain magma series was injected into the crust. Mt. Lafayette is the core of one such magma dike.

But the White Mountains of that time did not look like the White Mountains of today. It took millions of years of erosion to produce the topographic surface we see now.

Some fairly recent (perhaps 10 million years ago) uplifting caused mountainside streams to accelerate and cut deep ravines, such as Ammonoosuc Ravine. But by the beginning of the Pleistocene, a short 2 million years ago, the landscape appeared much as it does today.

It took only the cold, icy climate of the Pleistocene to smooth out some of the roughness.

Two kinds of ice action were involved—the areawide scraping by the great continental ice sheets, and the localized scouring by valley glaciers. The valley glaciers came first. As snow piled up in the leeward ravines, as it does in Tuckerman today, accumulations became so great that the snow persisted throughout the year. Under pressure of many years' pileup, snow at the bottom became ice and slowly oozed down-valley. Tuckerman's glacier filled the valley, joined with the one from Huntington Ravine, and flowed down almost to Pinkham Notch. The ice scoured out the valleys to a U-shape with steep headwalls at the upper end.

The Pleistocene may seem rather remote to us. But we are probably still in the tail end of one of the great ice surges. Indeed, if the average summer temperature were to decrease only a few degrees, perhaps 10, it is likely that Tuckerman Ravine would once again sport a glacier.

The continental ice sheets, on the other hand, covered the entire area, probably to a depth of a mile even at the top of Mt. Washington. The ice advanced from the northwest, sliding up and over the mountains, grinding away at the surface as it went. Surface striations and scourmarks are evident on exposed bedrock everywhere. The ice was channeled by the larger gaps in the mountains; Crawford Notch's U-shape is clear evidence that the continental ice sheet was at work.

Although the advancing ice scoured the rocks clean, it was really a dirty old glacier; and when it melted, it left its dirt behind. This glacial till, as it is called, is everywhere. It covers New Hampshire to an average depth of 32 feet, but the depth in the White Mountains is much less than that, generally only a foot or two. Glacial till can be recognized by the unstructured deposit of coarse sand and angular stones of all sizes. There really has been very little time for deep soils to form since the area was last covered by ice, perhaps 12,000 years ago. Most of the mountains' soils are therefore little-modified remnants of the glacial debris.

The continental glaciers produced other topographic oddities: erratic boulders carried from afar and dropped wherever the ice stopped its advance and melted; sheep-backs, low rounded bits of bedrock smoothed on the side from which the ice came and rough on the lee side; larger peaks similarly smooth on one side, rough on the other because of "plucking" of rocks from the summit by the advancing ice; and small lakes, called glacial tarns, scooped out by the ice.

Evidence of current "ice age" activity can be seen in the polygonal nets of rocks on flat areas above timberline and similar stone stripes on moderate slopes. Stones arrange themselves in U-shaped lobes on steeper slopes. All of these phenomena result from frost action in the stony glacial till.

A traverse of the central part of the White Mountains from one end of the hut system to the other reveals the surface evidence for the geological history outlined above. All of the features described and many more can be seen along the trail. The cross-section on page x-ref shows the route from Lonesome Lake to Carter Notch Hut, generally

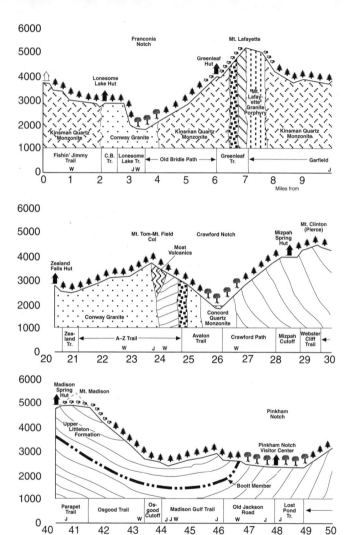

These cross-sections are taken along the AT and show the various bedrock formations that constitute the White Mountains. On the west, from Lonesome Lake to Crawford Notch, the dominating rocks are the granites formed from

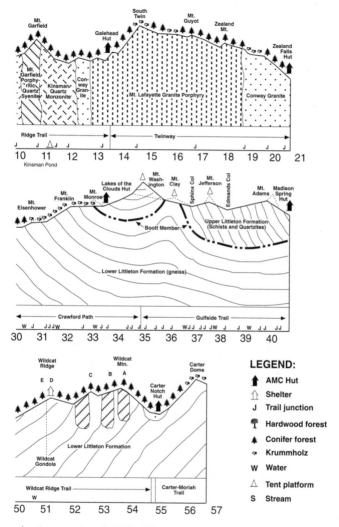

LEGEND:

🔺	AMC Hut
⬆	Shelter
J	Trail junction
🌳	Hardwood forest
🌲	Conifer forest
🌿	Krummholz
W	Water
△	Tent platform
S	Stream

volcanic magma intruded 150 million years ago. To the east, from Crawford Notch to Carter Notch, the upper and lower Littleton formations predominate. These were laid down as ocean sediments 350 million years ago.

following the Appalachian Trail, and indicates the bedrock geology traversed. Because it is a cross-section along the trail and thus winds around as does the trail, it is rather different from the typical geological cross-section. Little attempt is made to indicate the subsurface structure of the bedrock, except in the Presidentials where the structure is relatively simple.

Geologic features that may be studied in the vicinity of the huts are discussed in the individual hut chapters. Here only a brief overview of the major formations that are traversed is given.

At the westward end, the route crosses granites and porphyries of the White Mountain magma series and the quartz monzonites of the late Devonian intrusions. These were on the western side of the Presidential dome and were exposed as overlying rocks were eroded away. At Crawford Notch, the metamorphosed sediments of the Littleton formation are encountered. The Crawford Path is on the lower part of the formation, the upper part having been eroded away. At Monroe Flat, just before reaching the Lakes of the Clouds Hut, the tilted exposure of the Boott member is crossed and the trail enters the upper member of the Littleton formation. Because of folding and subsequent erosion, the Boott member is crossed twice in the vicinity of Mt. Clay (see diagram on page 27). The northern end of the high peaks is all on the upper part of the formation.

Just before reaching Pinkham Notch, the trail again crosses the Boott member and reenters the lower Littleton formation, which it follows all the way to Carter Notch.

Numerous signs of glacial activity are evident all along the way, especially above timberline. The alert walker will see this evidence everywhere.

3
Vegetation and Ecology

▼

TO the casual observer, the vegetation in an area seems terribly permanent; the changes from year to year are so slow as to be nearly imperceptible. A tree may increase in diameter a half-inch in a good growing season—fast growth for the tree but too slow to be perceived by the unaided eye. Sometimes changes are more rapid: a rock slide lays bare a portion of a hillside and piles loose rock and soil in a chaotic jumble bare of vegetation. In a year or two, something usually starts to grow on the bare soil, perhaps ragweed and other weeds. Soon goldenrod or pokeweed and a tangle of brambles take over, then such woody species as red maple or birch. Such changes are rapid in terms of ecological succession; but nevertheless it may be many years before the slope is once again covered with tall trees.

The overall impression is one of great stability—nothing seems to change very much. At low elevations, oaks may dominate the landscape for many years. Near timberline, balsam fir and red spruce may settle in and seem to be prepared for a long stay—perhaps forever. Ecologists have called these apparently permanent associations of trees the "climax" forest. It was thought to be the forest that would inevitably occupy an area after a sufficiently long period of time had elapsed.

On a time scale that is appropriate to the life span of forest trees, the environment is in an extraordinary state of flux. The weather changes not only from year to year, but also on time scales of decades, centuries, and millennia. The climate is always either warming up or cooling down. Indeed, it may be doing both at the same time; whether the climate is warming or cooling depends on the scale of the observation. For example, from 1940 to 1970, there was a general downward trend in the average temperatures of the northern hemisphere. But in the periods from 1950 to 1953 and from 1956 to 1960 temperatures increased. Some plants may respond to the longer-term variations, others may respond to shorter-term fluctuations. Still others may respond to factors other than temperature in ways we do not fully understand.

Other aspects of the plant environment also change and on various time scales. Forest fires can lay waste thousands of acres. Before the Europeans came, fires may have been started by the Indians or perhaps by lightning, although lightning fires are rather infrequent in New England. Some fires may be severe, killing nearly all the vegetation; others may be light, killing the ground vegetation but leaving the trees alive. Any one location is likely to be affected by a fire only once every hundred years or so.

New England is subject to devastating hurricanes and other severe storms. High winds can break or uproot and blow down individual trees or push over a small patch of timber. Full-fledged hurricanes can devastate thousands of acres, producing an impenetrable tangle of jackstraws. But again, any one area might experience such devastating winds only once every several centuries.

Still other forces are at work: insects and diseases can become epidemic on irregular cycles and may even wipe out entire tree species. The American chestnut was one of the Northeast's most magnificent trees until the chestnut blight eliminated it from our forests.

Even the seeds that fall on a patch of bare ground will come from different places at different times. Although atmospheric circulation patterns may remain more or less stable for many centuries, the winds that bring seeds to a barren patch of earth vary from day to day. The seeds brought in by ground animals and birds will not be the same from one year to the next. The distribution of seeds depends on the animals present at any one time.

The vegetation occupying a mossy glen, a patch of tundra, or a rocky hillside is in a dynamic state of flux, responding to the various forces that produce its environment. At the same time, the vegetation itself changes the environment, often modifying the microenvironment in such a way as to preclude its own continued existence there.

Is there such a thing as climax forest in the White Mountains? Probably not, although there are stands of virgin forest scattered about. If the term "virgin forest" is taken to mean a forest that has suffered no direct disturbance by humans, then there is virgin forest at the very upper limits of tree growth, extending into the krummholz—the low, matted vegetation just at timberline. But most of the White Mountains has been logged, some areas several times. And even areas that were not logged were probably culled by the early settlers for some of the best trees. One such area has been preserved by the U.S. Forest Service in Gibbs Brook Scenic Area, east of Crawford Notch. It contains numerous large spruce trees with diameters greater than two feet at breast height. It comes as close to being virgin forest as any in the region covered by this guide. Nevertheless, it should probably be referred

Logging in the White Mountains, 1908. AMC Collection.

to as an "old growth" forest rather than a virgin forest. The
Crawford Path, described in Chapter 10, traverses a portion of the Gibbs Brook stand.

Walking through the forest or across the tundra, you
can see the irregular distribution of the vegetation—no
patch is exactly like any other. And yet there are dis-
cernible patterns. There is the birch-beech-maple forest or
the high-elevation spruce-fir forest, but these are human
abstractions, designed to help sort out the flood of floristic
impressions that would otherwise be overwhelming. The
reality is far from the abstraction: the forest is a dynamic
complex of plants and animals continually reacting to the
ever-changing environment and yet influencing the environment by its own presence. With this in mind, we can
take a brief look at the ecological history of New England
and of the White Mountains in particular.

The ecological history of New England is a short one: it
starts 18,000 years ago when the last great continental ice

sheet, having reached Long Island, started to melt away. The ice did not, of course, retreat; that is, it did not flow back northward. As the climate warmed, the southern edge of the sheet melted faster than it could be replaced by the still-advancing ice from the north. The warming trend, marked by a rise in sea water temperature, started about 15,000 years ago. Moist air from the Atlantic Ocean and the Gulf of Mexico was more likely to produce rain than snow. The ice sheet became thinner as warm rain fell on the surface, melting it and carrying the meltwater to the sea. A patchy mosaic of ice remnants and bare ground resulted. It was not long before vegetation, from seeds brought in by birds, animals, or the wind, started to occupy the bare ground.

By 12,000 years ago, southern New England was mostly bare of ice. The landscape appeared much as it does today, with one major exception: there were no trees. The ground was covered with tundra vegetation. In northern New England, ice still covered the land, although the higher peaks were beginning to emerge. Ten thousand years ago, the ice margin was along the Gulf of St. Lawrence. Only remnants of valley glaciers remained in the White Mountains.

About this time, trees started to reinvade New England; spruce first, then pines and hemlocks along with hardy birches. White pines appeared about 9,000 years ago. Meanwhile, spruce and fir trees kept migrating northward, invading the tundra that developed as the ice melted. As the climate warmed, only the highest elevations could resist the invasion of the trees. Today, only a few square miles of tundra remain; most of it occupies elevations above 4,500 feet in the Presidential Range. Below the tundra, down to about 2,500 feet, lies the spruce-fir forest.

And in the lower valley, the hardwood forest of beech trees and various birches and maples is found. At still lower elevations, principally in the Connecticut River Valley, the forest consists primarily of white pine and hemlock, with hardwood species mixed in.

In the central White Mountains, there are three major ecological associations: the northeastern spruce-fir forest, the northern maple-beech-birch forest, and the alpine tundra.

A forest is classified as being in the maple-beech-birch ecosystem when 50 percent or more of the stand is composed of these three species, either singly or in combination. Common associates include hemlock and white pine. In the White Mountains, the dominant maple is the sugar maple. Birch is represented primarily by yellow birch, and there is only one native species of beech. The smaller trees are commonly mountain and striped maple, mountain ash (not really an ash but with ashlike compound leaves), and red maple in wet sites. Hobblebush, with its characteristic sprays of large paired leaves arranged along a long stem, is perhaps the most characteristic low plant seen along the trails. The association occupies an elevation range from 1,000 to 2,500 feet.

The northern spruce-fir forest ecosystem is characterized by a predominance of red spruce and balsam fir, mostly in mixed stands. It starts at an elevation of about 2,000 feet. The boundary is not sharp, and there is considerable intermixing with the lower hardwoods in an elevation band of about 500 feet. Common associates include hemlock, white pine, white birch, and, in a few locations, heart-leaved birch. At the upper limits, the spruce is likely to be black spruce, which often is a prominent species of the krummholz. Flowering plants on the forest floor include goldthread, bunchberry, mayflower, and a considerable variety of lilies such as clintonia and trillium. As timberline is approached, the trees become noticeably dwarfed, but still maintain their upright posture. This occurs at an elevation of about 4,200 feet. In exposed locations at an elevation of about 4,800 feet, true krummholz is found.

Timberline is defined as the upper altitudinal or latitudinal limit of upright trees. In the White Mountains this limit varies between about 4,800 and 5,200 feet in elevation, depending on exposure. Where snows are deep and slopes protected from wind, timberline is higher than on the windward slopes. It is a more nearly continuous line in the White Mountains than it is in the western mountains, where the true tundra is often interlaced with patches of high-lying trees. In all, about eight square miles of the White Mountains are occupied by tundra, most of it along the crest of the Presidential Range.

According to naturalist L. C. Bliss, about 110 species of higher plants are found above timberline, a rather small number. About 75 of these are true tundra plants and four are found almost exclusively in the White Mountains. Many have showy flowers, one of the great attractions of the Presidential Range. The early-season hiker is rewarded with spectacular displays of Lapland rosebay, bog laurel, moss campion, and alpine azalea. By July, most of the showy flowers are gone.

For the hiker interested in alpine flowers, two field manuals are essential: the *AMC Field Guide to Mountain Flowers of New England* and L. C. Bliss's *Alpine Zone of the Presidential Range.* Both are available at Pinkham Notch Visitor Center and at most of the huts.

To protect the trail and vegetation in wet spots, bog bridges are constructed out of logs. Lou Lainey.

As the cross section diagram (on pages 26–27) shows, all of the high huts lie in the spruce-fir forest or in the tundra. Only Pinkham Notch, at an elevation of 2,000 feet, lies in the hardwood forest. A traverse of the entire string of huts never drops lower than 1,800 feet. And only two other sections of the traverse, in Crawford and Franconia notches, are in the hardwood forest.

So a visit to the huts is a visit to the spruce-fir forest or the tundra above, a chance to see the dynamics of post-glacial forest succession at work, and a chance to study the wild beauty of the Arctic tundra.

4
Pinkham Notch Visitor Center

LOCATED at the height-of-land in Pinkham Notch, on what today is Route 16, the first Pinkham Notch Camp was a far cry from today's establishment. The log cabins built in the notch in 1920 followed the huts at Madison Spring, Carter Notch, and Lakes of the Clouds. It became obvious to the AMC hut committee that a central unit was needed to coordinate the operation of the three high huts then in existence, so two log cabins were built. There was a road through the notch at the time, but it was just a gravel track that was closed in the winter.

The major event of the early years at Pinkham, and the one that more than anything else sparked the development of a hut system, was the arrival in 1922 of Joe Dodge. He was the first full-time, year-round huts manager and reigned over Pinkham (which was nicknamed Porky Gulch because of a porcupine infestation) until 1959. His vision, enthusiasm, perseverance, native ability, and, some say, his eloquent way with language, were responsible for the accomplishments of the ensuing decade. The years from 1927 to 1936 saw the system expand to include four new huts—Greenleaf, Galehead, Zealand Falls, and Lonesome Lake—and major improvements made to all of the other huts, including Pinkham Notch Camp.

Pinkham Notch Camp, also known as "Porky Gulch," in 1926.
AMC Collection.

The original Pinkham Notch Camp was rather primitive. One of Dodge's first improvements was to build a roof over the washstands. This resulted in such an increase in their use that a new water line had to be laid. Prefabricated buildings were added in 1925 to replace the tents that had been used for sleeping quarters. And in 1927, the camp was kept open during the winter season. From then on there was a fury of construction, both at the notch and in the high country. The last major construction was Joe Dodge Lodge at Pinkham in 1973, containing guest quarters as well as a library, common room, and conference room.

Today Pinkham Notch Visitor Center (so renamed in 1990) has comfortable accommodations for more than a hundred guests in bunkrooms holding from two to six each. The modern kitchen and dining room, with its magnificent view of Wildcat Ridge, provide good food and pleasant surroundings for the family-style dinners and cafeteria-style breakfasts. The adjoining Trading Post carries a fairly complete inventory of backpacks, clothing, stoves, maps, guidebooks, and trail snacks. The basement contains washrooms and showers for the convenience of hikers who are not staying at the lodge.

Pinkham Notch Visitor Center is also the nerve center of the hut system. It is the largest of the huts and the only one (except for the Crawford Notch Hostel) that is accessible by road. Here all the supplies that are needed to provision the high huts are assembled, sorted, packaged, and prepared for delivery either to one of the pack houses at the trailhead near each hut, or to a helicopter landing pad for delivery by air. The 200-pound propane tanks—enough to last the summer—are airlifted in at the beginning of the

Pinkham Notch Visitor Center today. Lou Lainey.

season, and the empties are brought out the same way. (You may notice that most of the huts have a small landing pad, but you will probably never see a helicopter. Nearly all of the airlifting is done before or after the regular season.)

Most visitors to Pinkham Notch Visitor Center see only two buildings: the main building with its kitchen, dining room, and sales desk; and Joe Dodge Lodge containing the guest quarters and a conference room. But there is much more to Pinkham "out back." One building houses administrative offices. Another contains storerooms, walk-in refrigerators and freezers, and temporary bunkrooms for hut crews. Another houses the shops where much of the work of repairing and modifying the huts is accomplished. It is much easier to completely fabricate an item (a dish-drying cabinet, for example) here, then pack the pieces to the hut for assembly and installation, than it would be to pack in the raw materials and all of the tools necessary to do the work at the hut. Also made at Pinkham are the crews' packboards that are a trademark of the hut system.

Supplying the huts is a huge job. It is estimated that 50 tons of food, supplies, and hut-maintenance materials funnel through the Pinkham Notch warehouse every year. It is a logistical task that requires extraordinary managerial skill as well as a good physical plant to keep the materials moving in and out in an orderly fashion.

The director of facilities (formerly the huts manager) is able to maintain regular radio contact with all of the huts to provide weather information, inform crews of last-minute changes in guest lists, and provide a communication link in the event of a mountain injury. This is one reason why the huts are able to cope with such varied demands—from perhaps a dozen guests one night to a full house the next night. Hikers at the high huts often delay their departure until the 8 A.M. radio check that provides current weather forecasts, a matter not only of convenience but also of safety.

Pinkham Notch is also the base for the AMC hiker shuttle that makes regular runs to the trailheads and pack stations for all of the huts. Schedules are arranged so that it is possible to get from one trailhead to any other in a relatively short time. A current schedule can be obtained from the desk at Pinkham or by writing to the AMC and asking for *The Guide to AMC Huts and Lodges*. This informative bulletin also contains the current rates for lodging and meals at all of the AMC full-service facilities.

Pinkham Notch Visitor Center is the center for AMC's educational activities in the White Mountains. The AMC organizes and runs numerous workshops and conferences at the visitor center, often using the conference facilities in Joe Dodge Lodge. Evening programs of entertainment and education are held frequently in the dining room. Schedules are available at the sales and information desk.

Joe Dodge Lodge and Pinkham Notch Visitor Center, like all of the AMC huts, are open to the public. Reservations can be made by telephone (603-466-2727) or by writing to the Reservation Clerk, Pinkham Notch Visitor Center, Gorham, NH 03581. It is located on Route 16, 10 miles north of Jackson and 11 miles south of Gorham. A free parking lot uses a section of the old road and is open to all hikers. Pinkham Notch is a stop on the direct Concord Trailways bus route between Boston and Berlin. At present there is one round trip per day.

Geology

The Pinkham Notch area has much of geological interest. Many of the short walks described starting on page 44 lead to interesting geological formations.

The notch itself is underlain by the Littleton formation, the metamorphosed sediments that were laid down in the Devonian period. The so-called Boott member that separates the upper and lower parts of the Littleton formation passes through the notch and is exposed just below Crystal Cascade near the bridge over the Cutler River. The lower member of the Littleton formation is exposed in the series of cliffs along Route 16 just south of the Glen House. Exposures of the upper member can be seen in Tuckerman Ravine and Huntington Ravine (see cross section on pages 26–27).

The area was, of course, heavily glaciated by the continental ice sheet during the Pleistocene. The notch was scoured into its current U-shape by ice moving from the north. As the ice sheet withered away, it left many deposits of glacial till, which can be seen today in the road cuts along Route 16 north of the notch. The boggy area just across the road to the east of the visitor center may once have been a small pond formed by a depression in the till as the ice wasted away. It has since become filled by stream sediments from the sides of the notch. Beavers have reestablished a boggy pond in the area.

Glacial erratics abound. Glen Boulder, on a spur of Gulf Peak (sometimes called Slide Peak) and visible from Pinkham Notch, is an exceptionally large and spectacular example of such an erratic. It was probably picked up by the ice somewhere on Mt. Washington and dropped in its present location when the ice melted 10,000 years ago.

Ecology

Pinkham Notch Visitor Center, at an elevation of just over 2,000 feet, is the lowest of the AMC huts. Nevertheless, it is near the upper elevational limit of the northern hardwood association of birch, beech, and maple. A few feet higher, and the conifers of the spruce-fir forest enter in noticeable numbers.

Although the visitor center is located at the height-of-land in Pinkham Notch, the area is surprisingly well watered. A beaver pond directly across the highway contains an interesting variety of common bog plants, such as tall meadow-rue (*Thalictrum polygamum*), a member of the buttercup family with white flowers; the shrub sweetgale (*Myrica gale*); and speckled alder (*Alnus rugosa*). And, of course, the fascinating tundra vegetation of the Alpine Garden and Bigelow Lawn is readily accessible from Pinkham. Thus, the entire vegetational sequence from lowland bog to above-timberline tundra awaits the exploration of the Pinkham-based hiker.

Day Hikes from Pinkham Notch Visitor Center

There are numerous short walks in the Pinkham area—to spectacular viewpoints, interesting cascades, a tiny mountain lake, and just through some beautiful woods. (An excellent guidebook and large-scale map detailing walks in the Pinkham Notch vicinity is *Short Hikes and Ski Trips around Pinkham Notch,* by Linda Buchanan Allen and published by the AMC. It is available at the Trading Post.)

One of the most interesting walks is to Lost Pond, which sits on a bench hidden from the highway by a small knoll.

Lost Pond. The trail to Lost Pond (part of the Appalachian Trail) starts across the highway from the visitor center, about 70 yards south on Route 16. After a bridge crossing over the outlet of a beaver pond, the trail immediately turns south. Avoid the side trail (left) that leads to Square Ledge. The trail follows the east bank of the Ellis River for 0.3 mile, then swings left away from the river and climbs on a moderate grade to the pond. The trail follows the east shore of the pond, after which it descends slightly to the junction with the Wildcat Ridge Trail. Although there is no marked trail on the west side of the pond, it is a moderate scramble around the bluffs on the west side and back to the trail at the north end.

The forest along the trail and around the pond is a transition from the lower hardwoods to the spruce-fir forest of higher elevations. Here there is a large amount of birch mixed in with the balsam fir and red spruce. The pond appears to have been formed by rock slides from Wildcat Ridge in postglacial time. The resistant ridge of bedrock forming the eastern shore effectively stopped the slides and formed the small pocket now occupied by the lake. It is fed from underground springs and surface drainage from the slopes of Wildcat. Although rather shallow, it does not freeze solid in the winter and there are fish in it. Interesting marsh vegetation, such as red and painted trillium, star flower, Canada mayflower, and clintonia, occupies much of its shallow margins.

The round trip to the pond is about 1.5 miles and takes about an hour. Elevation gain is about 100 feet. Add a half-hour if you bushwhack around the west side.

Glen Ellis Falls. Glen Ellis Falls is undoubtedly the best-known waterfall in the White Mountains. Although

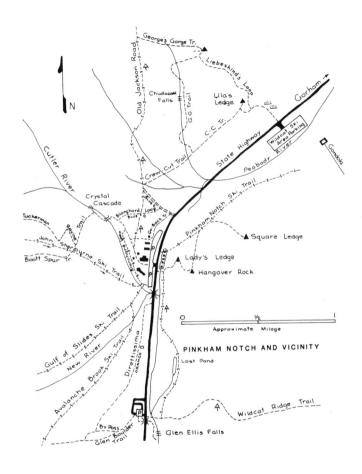

close to the highway (parking lot), the falls can be reached
from Pinkham on either of two trails: the Lost Pond Trail
described above or via the Direttissima on the west side of
the highway.

To reach the falls from the Lost Pond Trail (see above for trail description), go right at the junction with the Wildcat Ridge Trail and follow for 0.1 mile to the crossing (sometimes difficult in high water) of the Ellis River, just above the falls. Just before the tunnel under the highway, pick up the trail left that follows the west side of the river. (From the parking lot, enter the tunnel at the south end of the parking lot.) The trail follows down the west side of the Ellis River to the bottom of the falls, with outlooks along the way.

The Direttissima (derived from an alpinist's term for "most direct route") is marked partly with red paint blazes and partly with yellow, and parallels the west side of the highway. It starts at the south end of the highway bridge over the Cutler River (which then becomes the Ellis River) at a trail sign at the edge of the woods. This point is at the north end of an overflow parking lot. Just after entering the woods, it turns left (south) and soon enters a cleared area. At the end of the clearing, it swings west, then south, crossing a small brook. It skirts the upper end of a small gorge, crosses an unnamed brook on a bridge and soon reaches a viewpoint with a fine view down the notch. It then climbs a cliff, crosses another small brook and ends at the junction with the Glen Boulder Trail (sign), which you will take left (east). The trail drops sharply for a few yards and reaches the Glen Ellis parking lot in about 0.4 mile. The trail to the falls passes under the highway in a tunnel and reaches the falls in 0.1 mile.

Round trip to the falls is about 3 miles, and walking time is 1.5 hours.

Chudacoff Falls and Lila's Ledge. North of Pinkham Notch Visitor Center there are several interesting cascades and lookout points that can be visited by a net-work of trails. The route described climbs about 700 feet and has fine views of the ravines and ridges on either side of the notch. Although it can be taken in either direction, the best way is clockwise, up George's Gorge and down Liebeskind's Loop.

The route starts out on the Old Jackson Road (listed on some maps as Old Jackson Link), which branches right from Tuckerman Ravine Trail about 50 yards from its start at Pinkham. It is nearly level for the first 0.3 mile. Then it starts to ascend rapidly. After a stream crossing, the trail joins an abandoned section of the Old Jackson Road which enters from the right (sign). In a few yards, go right on the Crew-Cut Trail (it is called Brad's Trail on some signs),

Glen Ellis Falls is easily reached from Pinkham Notch. Jerry Shereda.

which is marked by blue blazes. After crossing a stony, dry brook bed, it runs generally east-northeast and crosses two more small brook beds; water may be found in the second of these. Just after this crossing (sign), take the George's Gorge Trail left, climbing steeply beside the Peabody River, which at this point is a small brook.

After crossing and recrossing the brook (Chudacoff Falls is visible from the second crossing), the George's Gorge Trail continues climbing on a rough and rocky trail to a junction where Liebeskind's Loop diverges right (sign). (Continue on George's Gorge Trail to the summit for a short spur trail to a lookout with fine views of Tuckerman and Huntington ravines to the west and Wildcat Mtn. to the east.)

Liebeskind's Loop (named for Steve Liebeskind, an AMC member who helped build the trail) descends to a swampy flat, then rises through a spruce thicket to the top of Casey's Cliff (called Brad Swan's Bluff on the 1989 Washburn map of Mt. Washington) with good views of Pinkham Notch. The trail then turns left, runs along the edge of the cliff, descends two gorges, and finally climbs a ridge. It swings southward to a shallow saddle (sign). Take the left branch for Lila's Ledge (called Brad & Lila's Ledge, after Brad and Lila Swan, on the 1991 map of Pinkham Notch), or the right branch for the most direct route back to Pinkham.

If you take the left branch, in 100 yards a sign indicates the route to the top of the ledge with its fine views of Pinkham and Wildcat Ridge. Retracing to the sign, an unmarked trail (right) can be taken straight down a few hundred yards to a junction with the Crew-Cut Trail. From this point, you can go right on the Crew-Cut Trail back to the Peabody River at the junction of George's Gorge Trail and then back to Pinkham the way you came.

Alternatively, follow the Crew-Cut Trail southeastward to a boggy bottomland and the junction with Connie's Way Ski Trail. Turn right and follow the ski trail to Old Jackson Road (sign), then left about 100 yards to the Go Back Ski Trail (sign), which is followed (right) to Pinkham.

Total trail distance is about 2 miles, with an elevation gain of 750 feet. Walking time is about 1.5 hours, not including time spent on the lookout points.

Crystal Cascade. Crystal Cascade, 0.3 mile from Pinkham Notch Visitor Center on the Tuckerman Ravine Trail, is of geologic interest for two reasons. The Boott member of the Littleton formation is exposed here, and the Cutler River cascades down a volcanic vent. The vent was active in the Mississippian period 300 million years ago. The volcanic rock here is diabase and it differs markedly from the metamorphic rocks of the surrounding Littleton formation. The diabase is dark gray or black and weathers to coarse, angular fragments. Another vent of typical basalt is exposed where the old bridge crossed the river a few yards downstream from the present bridge. It can be recognized by the dark angular fragments embedded in a dark greenish ground.

The Boott member is exposed below the base of the falls. Here it consists of light colored beds of actinolite schists and black biotite schist.

The cascades are reached via the Tuckerman Ravine Trail that leaves the visitor center area at the southwest corner of the Trading Post. It heads northwest on a broad footway. In 0.3 mile it crosses the Cutler River on the bridge mentioned above, turns right, and in a few yards reaches a side trail to the Cascade.

Round trip is 0.75 mile and is a 30-minute walk.

Square Ledge and Lady's Ledge. These ledges on the east side of Pinkham Notch provide fine views of Mt. Washington and its eastern ravines. Start out with the Lost Pond Trail (see above) but branch left on the Square Ledge Trail after crossing the footbridge. It climbs moderately, and after 80 yards, a spur path leads left to Lady's Ledge (called Lady's Lookout on the 1991 Pinkham Notch map) with a fine view of Pinkham Notch Visitor Center. The main trail bears right, swinging to the east, crosses the Square Ledge Loop Ski Trail, and then rises moderately, passing Hangover Rock. It then climbs to the base of Square Ledge, which it ascends steeply via a narrow slot to the outlook at the top.

Trail distance is about 1 mile, round trip. Allow 1 hour for the trip.

Mt. Washington via Tuckerman Ravine Trail. Although the Tuckerman Ravine Trail is not the shortest route to the summit of Mt. Washington—that distinction goes to the Ammonoosuc Ravine Trail–Crawford Path route—it is certainly the most spectacular and rewarding. It passes through the giant glacial cirque of Tuckerman Ravine, climbs the incredible headwall, and ascends the summit on the southeastern ridge. The climb can be combined with a trip through the Alpine Garden and its interesting geological and botanical displays.

The trail leaves Pinkham Notch Visitor Center at the southwest corner of the Trading Post where there is a pack scale and water fountain. After following a low ridge northeast of the Cutler River, it soon swings left and crosses the stream on a footbridge. It then turns right, follows the stream for a few yards, then turns left at a side trail right to Crystal Cascade (well worth a visit; see description above). The trail then ascends gradually, turning right where the Boott Spur Trail diverges left. It climbs on two long switchbacks, then continues westward. About 1 mile from Crystal Cascade, the Huntington Ravine Trail diverges right, and after crossing two tributaries, the unsigned Huntington Fire Road branches right. In 0.5 mile, the Raymond Path enters from the right. Here the Tuckerman Ravine Trail turns sharply left, quickly reaching the junction with the Boott Spur Link, which diverges left, and the Lion Head Trail, which diverges right. Hermit Lake and the Hermit Lake shelters are just beyond. Just above the shelters on a nearly level area are two buildings: a Forest Service snow rangers' cabin and the AMC Tuckerman cabin where the caretaker for the shelters lives. Trail and weather information are available here; although there is no longer a warming room, there is a large porch affording shelter from a sudden shower.

The main trail keeps to the right of Cutler River and ascends on a moderate grade to the floor of the ravine. At the foot of the headwall, it bears right and ascends a steep talus slope past where the Snow Arch usually forms on the left and persists into early summer. The sign here warning hikers from venturing near, under, or on the arch *must* be heeded. The arch has a nasty way of letting go with no warning. Tons of ice can cascade down, trapping even the wary hiker.

The trail climbs the right side of the headwall on a very steep and bouldery trail, finally turning sharply left at the top of the slope and traversing across a narrow ledge, a dike intruded into the Littleton formation. It then climbs straight up the slope at the top of the headwall. At this point, the Alpine Garden Trail diverges right on a contour. After climbing the grassy and ledgy slope for several hundred feet, Tuckerman Junction is reached at the top. Tuckerman Crossover leads straight ahead to Lakes of the Clouds Hut; the Lawn Cutoff leads south (left) to the Davis Path on Boott Spur; the Southside Trail leads northwest around the summit to the Davis Path near its junction with the Crawford Path; and the Tuckerman Ravine Trail, which you take, turns right to ascend the summit. The trail is marked by cairns (carefully piled rocks) and paint blazes on the rocks. It passes the junction with the Lion Head Trail at Cloudwater Spring in a few hundred yards and reaches the auto road just below the summit parking lot.

For the return trip via the Alpine Garden, follow the auto road to the Huntington Ravine Trail junction just below the 7-mile marker. (The trail sign is a short distance off the road.) Take this for 0.6 mile to the junction with the Alpine Garden Trail, which is followed right. The trail heads southward on a gentle descent across the beautiful Alpine Garden with its proliferation of tundra plants (best seen in June and early July) and interesting erosional features. After passing the junction with the Lion Head Trail, it contours along the top of Tuckerman Ravine to Tuckerman Junction. Here the Tuckerman trail is followed left back down Tuckerman Ravine to Pinkham Notch Visitor Center.

Trail distance up is 4.1 miles, elevation gain is 4,300 feet, and climbing time is 4.5 hours. The return trip via the Alpine Garden is 6 miles. Total round-trip time, excluding time on the summit, is 8 hours.

Access to Adjacent Huts

Pinkham Notch Visitor Center is located about midway on the base of an imaginary triangle joining Madison Spring Hut with Lakes of the Clouds Hut and Carter Notch Hut. Each of the three huts can be reached readily from Pinkham Notch in a half-day's walk.

Lakes of the Clouds Hut via Tuckerman Ravine Trail. This route, which takes about 4 hours, is described above; when you get to Tuckerman Junction, the Tuckerman Crossover leading straight ahead is followed across Bigelow Lawn. From the western edge of the "lawn," the hut can readily be seen. The trail drops quickly, joining the Crawford Path and the Camel Trail just above the first lake. The hut is reached in about 100 yards.

Carter Notch Hut via Wildcat Ridge Trail. This is the most direct route from Pinkham Notch to Carter Notch, although it is an arduous trip. The trail, which is 7 miles long and takes 6.5 hours, is described on page 219.

An alternate route that saves 2.25 miles and 3 hours of walking time is to take the Wildcat gondola to the ridge near the Wildcat D summit and pick up the Wildcat Ridge Trail at that point. See page 220.

Madison Spring Hut via Old Jackson Road and Madison Gulf Trail. The shortest, most protected route from Pinkham to Madison Spring Hut is up Madison Gulf. Although a moderate trail for most of the distance, the stretch up the headwall in Madison Gulf is very steep, requiring scrambling and the use of handholds, and may be slippery in wet weather. Stream crossings may be difficult in wet weather. Allow extra time and do not start up the headwall late in the day; it may take much longer than the estimated time.

The beginning of the route follows the white-blazed Old Jackson Road, which diverges right from the Tuckerman Ravine Trail about 50 yards from Pinkham Notch Visitor Center. This section is part of the Appalachian Trail. It passes the Crew-Cut Trail on the right, just after a bridge, and ascends steadily to the height-of-land where George's Gorge Trail branches right (this junction may be incorrectly signed Liebeskind's Loop). The trail descends slightly, crosses several brooks, and at a large brook takes a sharp left uphill. After a short steep climb, it levels off. The Raymond Path enters from the left, and after crossing several small brooks the Nelson Crag Trail also enters from the left. After climbing slightly, it crosses through a gravel pit and joins the auto road just above the 2-mile marker.

Madison Gulf Trail leaves the auto road immediately opposite, first climbing to a pass west of Lowe's Bald Spot. (A short side trail leads right to the viewpoint, with excellent views.) At the pass, the Madison Gulf Trail turns left, climbs slightly, and crosses open ledges with good views of Mt. Adams. It then drops sharply, crosses two brooks, then drops gently, crossing another brook before coming within sound of the West Branch of the Peabody River. It soon meets the Great Gulf Trail on the south bank (the two trails now run together for a short distance), turns sharp right, and descends steeply to the stream.

The trail crosses to the north bank on a suspension bridge and climbs the small ridge separating the stream just crossed from Parapet Brook. Here the Madison Gulf Trail (recently relocated) diverges sharply left up the narrow ridge and continues between the two streams until it enters its former route near the bank of Parapet Brook. It crosses one channel of the divided brook, runs between the two for 0.1 mile, then crosses the other to the northeast bank. It follows the brook bank for a little way, then turns right, away from the brook, then turns left and ascends along the valley wall at a moderate grade, coming back to the brook at the mouth of the branch stream from Osgood Ridge. From here it follows Parapet Brook rather closely and crosses the brook for the first of three times in less than 0.5 mile, ascending to the lower floor of the gulf where it reaches Sylvan Cascade at an elevation of 3,800 feet.

The trail now climbs to the floor of Madison Gulf, at an elevation of 4,000 feet, which it traverses, making four brook crossings. It rises gradually to Mossy Slide at the foot of the headwall, then steeply, with some difficult scrambles, up the headwall, following the stream. After passing through scrub, it comes out on the rocks and ends at the junction with the Parapet Trail.

The route now follows the Parapet Trail, left, over the Parapet, which it reaches in 100 yards. Madison Hut is 0.25 mile farther.

Trail distance is 6.25 miles, and the total climb is 3,300 feet. Walking time is 5 hours.

Winter at Pinkham Notch Visitor Center

For most skiers, winter at Pinkham Notch Visitor Center means one thing: skiing Tuckerman Ravine. Hardy skiers have been making pilgrimages to Tuckerman for more than half a century. The combination of a deep east-facing bowl and the southwest winds on which the heaviest snows are borne leads to huge snowpacks and ideal skiing conditions that last well into spring and early summer.

When the snow has disappeared in every other skiing area in New England, there is still Tuckerman Ravine.

It is not surprising that snow should accumulate to such a depth in the ravine, for it is the best developed glacial cirque in the White Mountains. Tuckerman Ravine and adjoining Huntington Ravine both had valley glaciers until about 50,000 years ago (after this the continental ice sheet obliterated the valley glaciers). They joined to form a single valley glacier in the Cutler drainage that reached almost to Pinkham Notch. With a slightly lower summer temperature (perhaps 10°) it is likely that a permanent snowfield would develop high in the ravines and new valley glaciers would form.

As it is, enough snow usually remains in the bowl to permit skiing until June. Often there is snow on the trail up the headwall well into June, forcing hikers to take the Lion Head Trail for the trek to the summit of Washington. The snow usually accumulates to sufficient depth to cover the rocks and permit skiing by late March. Then the bowl is one vast expanse of unbroken snow, with slopes ranging from nearly flat on the floor to frighteningly steep well up the headwall. Few but the most intrepid (some would say crazy) skiers attempt the steepest portions.

The incredible schuss of Toni Matt is a mountain legend. During the annual Inferno Race in 1939, Matt skied from the top of Mt. Washington to Pinkham Notch in 6.5 minutes, going straight over the Tuckerman headwall. It is not a feat to be recommended.

The slopes are sufficiently steep and the snow accumulations so great that there is considerable avalanche hazard, especially early in the season. The U.S. Forest Service maintains a snow ranger at Hermit Lake to monitor

the hazard. Some control work is done and the skiing conditions are communicated to Pinkham Notch Visitor Center where they are posted on a status board outside the
Trading Post. The various ravines and slopes may be
closed to skiing at times by the Forest Service. The clos-
ings must be rigidly observed. But from late March on,
skiing conditions are frequently ideal, and a steady stream
of skiers trudge up the trails to the bowl every morning.
Good weekends may find a thousand skiers jockeying for
position in the bowl, which is remarkable considering that
there is no lift and no way to get there but by walking. For
the way down, there is the John Sherburne Ski Trail that
parallels the hiking trail. The trail is good until late in the
season when the snow has left the lower elevations.

Skiing in Tuckerman Ravine is true alpine skiing.
There are also many good cross-country trails in the immediate vicinity of Pinkham, trails to suit all categories of
skiers.

Trail distance to the Tuckerman shelter is 2.5 miles
with an elevation gain of 1,800 feet. The floor of the bowl
is 0.3 mile farther and nearly 500 feet higher. Walking
time to the bowl is about 3 hours.

Ski-Touring Trails

If spring at Pinkham Notch is given over to Tuckerman
headwall aficionados, winter is the province of the cross-
country skier. Touring trails abound in the notch. They are
covered fully in *Short Hikes and Ski Trips Around
Pinkham Norch* referred to previously.

5
Lonesome Lake Hut

From the Hut Log: July 15, 1952

> Arrived in time to help demolish a damn fine roast beef and accessories. Spent night and most of morning reluctant to return to inferno below (record heat wave, according to radio). Thanks to hut management (Pete and Hal) for most lavish food and quarters in over a week.
>
> **Marge and Dave Jeffries**
> Boston wharf rats

LONESOME Lake Hut overlooks a beautiful glacial tarn. Perhaps the best thing about the lake for the tired hiker is that it is shallow and warms up quickly in the spring. A refreshing swim is the perfect way to end a hot day's hike. The walk from the highway in Franconia Notch is short and easy, so Lonesome Lake is a favorite with family groups.

The original cabin at Lonesome Lake was built in 1876 by W. C. Prime, at the time a well-known author. When the state of New Hampshire acquired the land for Franconia Notch State Park in 1929, the lake and the cabin were included. The cabin was leased to the AMC to serve as one of its growing string of backcountry huts. However, the cabin needed renovation and some addition before it was suitable for hut use. By the summer of 1930, a kitchen and dining area had been built, and the hut was ready for visitors. Situated on the northeast shore of the lake, the hut had fine views of Kinsman Ridge.

When Lafayette Place Campground was established, New Hampshire expected that Lonesome Lake would serve as its swimming facility. The cool waters of the lake apparently did not entice many campers to undertake the 1.5-mile hike; in 1964, in an attempt to increase patronage, New Hampshire built a refreshment stand on the south shore. For whatever reason, the state immediately leased the structure to the AMC. Two additional buildings were constructed as bunkhouses. The decaying structures at the north end of the lake were torn down; their location just north of the trail junction can still be identified.

In 1979, New Hampshire tired of maintaining the complex and gave the whole business to the AMC. The main building, an octagonal structure, houses the kitchen and dining room; crew quarters are attached in a wing that stretches west from the octagon. Two buildings nearby hold sleeping quarters for 46 people in a series of small bunkrooms.

Lonesome Lake Hut. Paul Mozell.

Lonesome Lake Hut in the early 1960s. William Bardsley/AMC Collection.

Geology

Lonesome Lake sits in a small, shallow basin below the arc of peaks formed by Mt. Kinsman, Kinsman Ridge, and Cannon Mtn. It was scooped out during the Pleistocene epoch by the continental ice sheet that ground its way southward over the White Mountains. The lake is at an elevation of 2,734 feet, just 1,000 feet higher than Franconia Notch, a scant mile to the east. It is about 0.3 mile long and is 0.1 mile wide and has a surface area of about 80 acres. The depth of the lake averages 3 to 6 feet with the greatest depth, about 12 feet, just off the southwest shore. The bedrock under Lonesome Lake is Conway granite, a medium-grained, pink biotite granite that is ubiquitous in the White Mountains. The granite surrounding the lake has weathered to a whitish color flecked with grains of gray quartz and black flakes of biotite mica. The sandy, granular material found on the Lonesome Lake Trail consists of particles weathered from the granite. Outcrops of Conway granite can also be seen along this trail.

At the southwest end of the lake, the bedrock is Kinsman quartz monzonite. The many large crystals of potash feldspar distinguish it from the uniformly grained Conway granite. These crystals, called phenocrysts, were formed when the molten mass that formed the granite cooled very slowly. The phenocrysts in the rocks near the hut range in size from one to two inches in length. The monzonite matrix is darker than the Conway granite, and the feldspar crystals stand out.

Although the lake itself sits on acidic rock and is nearly surrounded by acidic bogs, the water is barely acidic. The water flowing into the lake comes largely from Kinsman Ridge with its feldspar crystals. Weathering of the feldspar leads to an influx of soluble calcium, which exerts a strong buffering action, neutralizing much of the acid from the bogs and granite. Even the input from acid rain is well buffered and the lake supports a large stock of brook trout, unusual for many of the nearby lakes.

Much of the soil mantle covering the bedrock near Lonesome Lake Hut is glacial till, a mixture of stones, sand, and clay deposited by the glacier. It can be seen almost anywhere a shallow excavation is made; there are several close to the buildings.

The sharp-edged boulders that lie in profusion in the area are glacial erratics, boulders that have been moved to the area and deposited by the melting glacier. Most of these were torn from the two bedrock types present. An occasional erratic from a different bedrock can also be found.

The terrain surrounding the lake is typical of recent continental glaciation: rounded ridges with shallow depressions filled with thin layers of glacial till and erratic boulders. The U-shaped notch and valley just to the north of the lake are typical of heavily glaciated terrain.

Ecology

The area around Lonesome Lake has two interesting ecological stories to tell. One is the ecological succession in shallow ponds; the other is the succession of plants that follows a major disturbance of the land, in this case extensive logging.

The lake itself was probably a very shallow beaver pond and bog before the loggers came. The lake level was raised and stabilized by a small dam near the outlet which has recently been replaced by a pressure-treated fir dam. If you look closely, an underlying concrete dam can be seen. At present, there are no beavers in the lake area. A short way below the outlet, however, recent activity can be seen. The largest dams are on the northwest side of the lake, including one that is nearly 0.3 mile long. Beavers have built a series of dams upstream from the northwest shore, creating shallow ponds at successively higher levels.

The bog along the west and northwest shores can be reached by a path that goes completely around the lake. Most of the boggy areas have been bridged by logs and plank walkways, making it possible to traverse the bog and study it closely. (An excellent guide to this trail, *Lonesome Lake Nature Guide,* by E. Dean and A. Lukens, describes the flora and fauna around the lake. Although it is now out of print, a loan copy may be available at the hut. It should be consulted by anyone wishing to learn more about the natural history of the Lonesome Lake area.)

The forest surrounding Lonesome Lake is predominantly red spruce (*Picea rubens*) and balsam fir (*Abies balsamea*). They are easily distinguished: balsam needles are arranged in flat sprays whereas red spruce needles come from all sides of the central stalk. The spruce branchlet also feels sharp and spiny when grasped in the hand.

The paper birch growing in the vicinity of the lake is heart-leaved birch (*Betula papyrifera var. cordifolia*), a variety of American white birch. It has a heart-shaped leaf rather than the more common oval shape of the main species. Otherwise it is nearly indistinguishable from white birch. American mountain ash (*Pyrus americana*), also common in the area, has only its leaf shape in common with the true ashes. It is a shrub or small tree that has compound leaves (with leaflets paired along the leaf stem). But the leaf stems alternate along the branchlets; true ash leaf stems are arranged opposite each other.

The birch, a favorite of the beaver, is a pioneer species that quickly springs up after a major disturbance such as a fire. Although gradually overtopped by the slower-growing spruce and fir, it may remain in the understory for many years, adding visual variety to the otherwise dark forest.

A guided nature walk at the end of this chapter describes many of the area's unique features.

Access to the Hut

Lonesome Lake Hut is the westernmost hut of the string along the Appalachian Trail (AT). It lies about halfway between Kinsman Pond and the point where the AT crosses the road in Franconia Notch. The shortest route to the hut is not the AT, however, but the Lonesome Lake Trail, which starts at Lafayette Place Campground. (Lafayette Lodge, near the entrance to the campground, has a grocery store.)

Via Lonesome Lake Trail. The trail leaves Lafayette Place Campground at the parking lot at the south end of the picnic area near the southbound exit of I-93 (the Franconia Notch Parkway). There is also a parking lot at the northbound exit, 3.5 miles north of the Flume; a walking

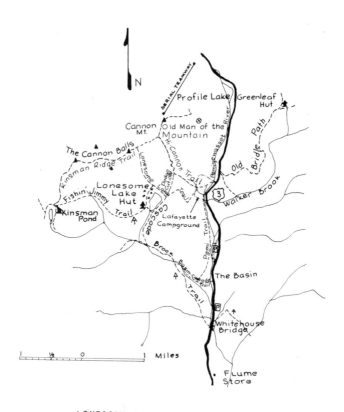

Map labels:

N

AERIAL TRAMWAY

Profile Lake

Greenleaf Hut

Cannon Mt.

Old Man of the Mountain

The Cannon Balls

Kinsman Ridge Trail

W. Cannon Trail

Pemigewasset River

Old Bridle Path

Lonesome Lake Trail

Cannon Trail

Lonesome Lake Hut

Fishin' Jimmy Trail

Kinsman Pond

Cascade Trail

Walker Brook

3

Lafayette Campground

Brook

Basin Cascade Trail

Cascade Brook Trail

Pemi Trail

The Basin

Miles

Whitehouse Bridge

Flume Store

LONESOME LAKE HUT AND ENVIRONS

tunnel under the highway provides trail access. (Note: The
parking lots are unsupervised, and hiker parking, though
free and unlimited, is at the parker's risk.)

After crossing the Pemigewasset River on a footbridge, the trail heads west through the campground fol-

lowing yellow paint blazes. It enters the woods between campsites 93 and 95 on the upper campground road, just opposite a water hydrant. Here it swings left on predominantly level terrain for a short distance, then it starts to climb diagonally up a moderate slope. After crossing a small stream on a footbridge, the path quickly reaches the junction of the Hi-Cannon Trail, which diverges right. The Lonesome Lake Trail continues to climb moderately on three long switchbacks to a broad height-of-land. Just before reaching the lake, a trail junction is reached. The Dodge Cutoff branches right to join the Hi-Cannon Trail. The Cascade Brook Trail leads left to the hut along the eastern shore of the lake. A wide flat path is followed to the lake's outlet, which is crossed on the Fishin' Jimmy Trail just below the small dam. In a few yards, the trail veers left away from the lake and climbs to the main hut.

The distance from the footbridge at Lafayette Place Campground to the hut is 1.75 miles; the total climb is 900 feet. Walking time is about 1.5 hours.

Via Cascade Brook Trail. The Cascade Brook Trail, a link in the AT, also leads from the highway to Lonesome Lake. It is a longer but gentler walk.

Day Hikes from Lonesome Lake Hut

The visitor to Lonesome Lake Hut has a choice of several interesting loops, ranging from a short walk around the lake to a full-day trip to the Cannon Balls and Cannon Mtn. For the naturalist, the short walk around the lake may be the most rewarding. From it, you can see the forces of the natural environment interacting with and shaping the plant and animal life that inhabit the area. Ecological succession is active here—a shallow pond is rapidly (by ecological standards) being transformed into dry land. Beavers actively assisted this transition. A trip around the lake is a fascinating experience for anyone who walks the trail with open eyes (see self-guided nature walk at the end of this chapter).

Round trip to Kinsman Pond and the Cannon Balls. Don't be fooled by the mileage on this loop—only 6.5 miles—nor by the apparently easy climb to the eastern-most Cannon Ball—only 1,000 feet above the lake. The ridge is like a roller coaster, and before the day is out you will have climbed at least an additional 2,000 feet. Nevertheless, it is an interesting trip through the high-altitude spruce-fir forest, with some fine views from the rounded summits of the Cannon Balls. Good training for the Garfield Ridge Trail.

From the hut, follow the Cascade Brook Trail around the east side of the lake (the west side is a little shorter but may be rather boggy and wet in spots). Pick up the Lonesome Lake Trail at the junction and follow it north of the lake. At the northernmost point, the trail along the west shore enters from the left. This portion may be boggy and does not have the advantage of the log bridges on the west-side trail. The trail rises gently at first, then more steeply, reaching the Kinsman Ridge Trail at Coppermine Col, about 1 mile from the lake.

Follow the Kinsman Ridge Trail left, which climbs about 400 feet to the top of the easternmost and highest Cannon Ball (3,769 feet). The trail drops to a shallow draw and slabs the northwest side of the middle Cannon Ball, then drops further to a ravine where water can usually be found. (Water tends to be scarce on the ridge; carry a suffi-cient supply.) After climbing the westernmost Cannon Ball (3,693 feet), the trail drops about 100 feet and climbs another hump on the ridge before dropping to Kinsman Junction just north of Kinsman Pond. Continue straight about 100 yards to Kinsman Shelter. Kinsman Pond was discovered in 1871 by two members of the graduating class of Dartmouth College who were on a geological survey of the area. It would probably be little visited even today were it not for the presence of the Appalachian Trail. Please note that the pond water and the water in the spring near the shelter are not potable.

From Kinsman Junction, Fishin' Jimmy Trail, part of the AT, leads eastward, twice crossing the brook draining Kinsman Pond. It drops to a level spot, then drops again to another flat, which it traverses for about 0.2 mile, where water is usually found. The trail undulates gently until it reaches the Lonesome Lake Hut about 2 miles from Kinsman Junction. Incidentally, the Fishin' Jimmy Trail gets its peculiar name from the chief character in a story by Annie Trumbull Slosson, once a well-known regional author, who set the story's scene in this area.

As indicated earlier, the loop is about 6.5 miles long, climbs more than 2,000 feet, and will take about 6 hours of walking time. About half of this will be spent on the ridge between Coppermine Col and Kinsman Junction.

Cannon Mtn. Cannon Mtn.—sometimes called Profile Mtn.—is one of the most famous, probably the most stared-at of the White Mountains, for it harbors the Old Man of the Mountains on its eastern ledges. For skiers, it is better known for its aerial tramway to the summit, the first built in the United States. The summit also contains an observation tower on very nearly the highest point, and there is a restaurant at the top of the tramway. The tramway runs year-round, so there is likely to be a crowd of tourists on top. For the 4,000-footer buffs, Cannon Mtn. (4,100 feet) is easily climbed from Lonesome Lake.

From the Lonesome Lake Trail junction at the east end of the lake, follow the Dodge Cutoff for about 0.3 mile north to its junction with the Hi-Cannon Trail. Going left from here the Hi-Cannon Trail climbs steeply to an outlook with good views of Franconia Notch and Franconia Ridge to the east. In a few hundred yards, it passes the Cliff House, a natural rock shelter. The trail ascends a ladder, and passes along the top of the cliffs at the south end of the Cannon Mtn. ridge overlooking the lake. After a short but rough climb, the trail tops the ridge where it joins the Kinsman Ridge Trail. It follows this right, 0.4 mile to the summit.

For the return journey to Lonesome Lake, pick up the Kinsman Ridge Trail at the junction just north of the observation tower, and follow it south to the junction of the Hi-Cannon Trail. This is then followed down to the top of the ridge where the Dodge Cutoff diverges. This is followed in easy stages to the trail junction at the lake.

For a diversion, instead of taking the Hi-Cannon Trail, continue on the Kinsman Ridge Trail to Coppermine Col, where Lonesome Lake Trail heads southward to the Around-Lonesome-Lake Trail at the north end. Very little difference in time.

The round-trip mileage is about 5 miles, and the elevation gain is 2,300 feet. Time up about 2.5 hours, returning about 1.5 hours.

Access to Adjacent Huts

Greenleaf Hut. The shortest route from Lonesome Lake to Greenleaf Hut is via the Lonesome Lake Trail to the Lafayette Place Campground, then up the Old Bridle Path.

The Appalachian Trail follows a different route and actually does not lead to the hut but passes it to the east over the summit of Mt. Lafayette. The AT follows down Cascade Brook Trail, crosses I-93 at Whitehouse Bridge, then ascends Franconia Ridge on the Liberty Spring Trail. After gaining the ridge, it leads north on the Franconia Ridge Trail to Mt. Lafayette. From here, the Greenleaf Trail must be followed down (west) to the hut. The total distance is nearly 11 miles, and walking time is about 7 hours. For detailed trail descriptions of this route, the *AMC White Mountain Guide* should be consulted.

The short route follows the Around-Lonesome-Lake Trail along the west shore of the lake (or the Cascade Brook Trail along the east shore) to the trail junction at the easternmost point. From here, the Lonesome Lake Trail leads southeast (right) over a low saddle, then swings left down an increasingly steep slope. After reaching a small draw, it turns sharply right and begins a series of long switchbacks to Lafayette Place Campground. Crossing under the highway at the campground entrance, the route follows the Old Bridle Path past the trail information booth. The description of the Old Bridle Path to Greenleaf Hut can be found on page 81.

Trail distance from Lonesome Lake Hut to the highway is 1.6 miles, with an elevation loss of 900 feet. From the highway to Greenleaf Hut, the distance is 2.5 miles, with an elevation gain of 2,500 feet. Total walking time from Lonesome Lake Hut to Greenleaf Hut is 3.5 hours.

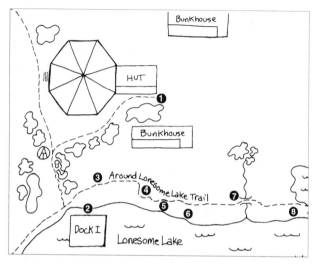

A Self-Guided Nature Walk
Lonesome Lake Hut
by Jan M. Collins

The area around Lonesome Lake is biologically rich and varied. Some plants are uncommon if not rare. All life is fragile and may take your lifetime or longer to replace. To preserve Lonesome Lake for your next visit, please stay on the trail and avoid picking or eating any plants or approaching any animals.

Station One

There are three small mammals commonly seen in the clearing in front of the hut. The chipmunk has five dark brown or black stripes from the shoulder to the tail, alternating with white stripes. It is primarily a ground dweller and will make its home in tunnels, old stumps, rotting logs, and under loose rocks. They are well known for their ability to stuff great quantities of food into their cheek pouches. The red squirrel nests in trees. It is larger and more aggressive than the chipmunk and is an excellent swimmer. Both chipmunks and squirrels commonly eat nuts, seeds, berries, and mushrooms. But they have been known to run off with candy bars or even whole sandwiches when unsuspecting visitors turn their backs. Beware. Our third resident, the snowshoe, or varying hare, is usually active in the morning or evening hours. It is brown in summer but will develop a white coat to match the snow in winter. Hares, unlike rabbits, give birth to young with fur, open eyes, and the ability to run shortly after birth.

Station Two

Leave the hut and descend to the dock at the lake. On a clear day you can look across the lake at the naked rocks of Franconia Ridge. Sometimes the mountains are veiled in low-lying clouds. As moist air is forced by air currents to climb the ridge, it condenses in the cool temperatures of the higher elevations. Sometimes you can actually watch the clouds form. At other times, the only clouds in a clear blue sky are those over the mountain.

Directly to your left are the Cannon Mtns. As glaciers flowed in a southerly direction, they pushed slowly up and over, polishing the north side of the mountains, then dropped on the south side, plucking rocks from the slope and creating the rough, steep ledges we see today. The force of the glacier's downward, southerly movement gouged out a basin as it hit more level land and created the large depression that now contains Lonesome Lake.

Station Three

As you move to the left around the lake, you will be walking along a series of split-log footbridges. After a spring rain, it is obvious that the bridges protect hikers from wet feet and muddy boots. But their real service is to protect the fragile wetland plants. Green sedges, shrubs, and herbs grow beneath and beside the logs. If the bridges were not there, the trail would be little more than a wide, muddy swath with vegetation trampled, dead, or dying. Most of the bog bridges, like much of the trail maintenance, are built by volunteer trail crews, people like you who are willing to spend a weekend or more giving back energy and time to the mountains. See the hut crew for more information.

Station Four

A hundred feet or so on the left, soon after crossing the black piping, you will notice a cluster of uprooted trees lying on their sides. Look closely and you will see the very shallow soil that held the tree roots in place. It is not hard to imagine how a slight rain and a good wind could easily topple these large trees. The ground underneath the roots is a jumble of granite rocks. Dragged for miles, these rocks were dumped here by the glacier that scraped away the topsoil and gouged out the lake basin. Shallow soil with granite bedrock near the surface prevents the growth of certain tree species, like maples, that require deep taproots for development. Shallow-rooted trees like spruce, fir, and birch thrive here.

Station Five

Bedrock near the surface can also limit water drainage and form wetlands in flat areas. On either side of the bog bridges are spread thick mats of sphagnum moss (also called peat moss). Along with the pale green sphagnum, you will find clumps of red sphagnum. This is a natural color variation and does not signify disease. Sphagnum is well known for its ability to absorb and retain huge amounts of water. If you can't distinguish sphagnum from other mosses, just reach down and give a clump a gentle squeeze. It is the only moss that will actually produce drips of water. Its acid content also inhibits bacterial growth, allowing it to survive water-saturated environments.

Station Six

At the end of one set of bog bridges, you will come to a perfectly flat sitting rock with a splendid view of Franconia Ridge on your right. Notice the deep V-shaped ravines carved in the flanks of the ridge. This characteristic deep V indicates weathering by water and tells us the primary shaping of the ravine has occurred since the glaciers receded 10,000 years ago. Valleys formed by glaciers are U-shaped. Franconia Notch is an example of a glaciated valley.

If you are sitting on the rock looking at the view, your back is turned on a colony of sundew plants (*Drosera rotundifolia*). These tiny little plants grow in a rosette with leaves that look like miniature spoons with sticky red hairs. The drops of sweet liquid at the end of each hair trap small unsuspecting insects. Wet soils are often deficient in nutrients for plant growth. The sundew gets nitrogen for growth by digesting insects.

On the bank above the sundew are two ground plants that look like the three leaves of a clover. Goldthread has shiny evergreen leaves with irregular margins. Gently poke your finger in the ground and follow its stem down to the roots. A little probing should reveal the source of the plant's name. Its roots look like a filament of gold thread. Gently re-cover the exposed roots.

Mountain wood sorrel also resembles clover, but its leaves are not shiny and have smooth margins. Sorrel means sour. If you could taste the leaf, you would understand immediately how it got it name.

Station Seven

Continue on the bog bridges until you reach an open meadow. Many of the trees are dead, probably from root rot, but the shrubbery remains incredibly lush. You are surrounded by plants characteristic of bogs. The grasslike plants are sedges and rushes. Sedges have edges (their stems are triangular), rushes are round. Just before you cross a small tributary on a double-logged bridge, turn right and face the pond. A tamarack should stand between you and the pond. It has short needles arranged in small clumps along its branches, giving it a fuzzy appearance. The tamarack, or larch, is the only conifer in the northeast to shed its needles in the fall. The needles turn a golden orange before dropping. In winter the skeleton of the tree stands naked. Without any needles it appears dead. In spring new needles will once again dress its branches.

A white pine stands alone on the left. It is distinguished from the spruce and fir that dominate this area by its long needles and prominently upturned branches.

Station Eight

If you continue to the far edge of the meadow where the trail reenters the spruce-fir forest, you will see on your left the remains of a beaver dam. Though the beavers have been removed from the area, the fruit of their labor continues to provide productive wetland habitat. Wetlands, where water and land meet, are the most biologically productive acreage on Earth. Nutrients in the soil mix with the water to provide food for microscopic organisms and water plants. These organisms are eaten by small insects and crustaceans and they in turn by even larger organisms including frogs, toads, salamanders, mice, voles, mink, foxes, hawks, owls, bears, and even moose. You may see black ducks paddling around with their tails straight up in the air and their heads poking about in the mud for underwater food. Black ducks are particularly attracted to beaver ponds for breeding. They, like moose, are indebted to the beavers for providing the shallow wetlands that encourage the growth of marsh grasses and weeds.

Besides providing ecological diversity, wetlands improve water quality by filtering pollutants and excess nutrients from such sources as farm runoff and waste water treatment plants that often contaminate surface water. They also act as a sponge to absorb and alleviate the destructive force of floodwaters by releasing them slowly. Several species of fish require shallow wetland waters for breeding and feeding. Small fish use the shallows to escape from larger predators. In the past, wetlands were considered useless breeding grounds for biting insects. As such, they were bulldozed and filled. Less than half of the wetlands that existed when Europeans arrived remain. That means the wetlands that survive are even more precious. Preservation is of the utmost importance.

6
Greenleaf Hut

———————◆———————

From the Hut Log: May 9, 1934

> Met two Dartmouth fellows climbing up in low shoes and
> business suits. Seems that they were a trifle discouraged.
> Nothing but wind and clouds.

Martin Bailey

GREENLEAF Hut was not the first building on Mt.
Lafayette. In the early days of White Mountain
tourism, it was fashionable to build hostels or small hotels
on accessible peaks. These were often constructed by the
proprietors of the grand hotels in the valleys as places
where their guests could rest after the arduous horseback
ride to the summit and further enjoy the glories of sunset
and sunrise from the top of the world. The history of the
Mt. Lafayette hostelry is somewhat obscure, but it was
probably built in the 1840s. Main access must have been
by horse, for there are remains of a corral and stable nearby. It did not last very long, for Moses F. Sweetser's *The
White Mountain Guidebook*, 1875 edition, indicates that
nothing was left but the stone walls. In common with most
of the mountaintop hotels of the day, and many of those in
the valleys, it was probably consumed by fire.

For 60 years there was no overnight shelter on Lafayette.
But in the late 1920s, Colonel C. H. Greenleaf, one of the pro-
prietors of the Profile House, a grand hotel in Franconia
Notch, left a sum of money to the Appalachian Mountain

Club that was used to construct a hut near Eagle Lakes. A plaque dedicating the hut to Col. Greenleaf can be found on the east-facing stone front, the one facing Mt. Lafayette.

Built in 1929, under the supervision of Joe Dodge, Greenleaf Hut was the first time donkeys were used to haul construction materials up the mountains. It was also the first hut with running water and inside toilets. The construction of Greenleaf represented a major change from the typical stone masonry of Madison and Lakes of the Clouds. The structure is wood-frame, which makes for a warmer and less damp hut. The interior design also represented a departure from the previous designs. The central portion contains the kitchen and common room; two wings off the common room contain the bunkrooms. Originally these were designated as a men's bunkroom and a women's bunkroom; but today they are more or less integrated, depending on the make-up of the night's guest list. A major reconstruction in 1989 upgraded the kitchen and expanded the common room. There are bunks for 48, and

Greenleaf Hut, looking west toward the Old Bridle Path. Paul Mozell.

it is run by a crew of five. The hut is operated as a full-service facility from early June to early September, but is open with a caretaker in residence from mid-May and after the regular season until mid-October.

Greenleaf is one of the busiest huts of the system because the climb of Mt. Lafayette and the traverse of Franconia Ridge are second only to the ascent of Mt. Washington in popularity. A good day, especially on weekends, will find dozens if not hundreds of hikers making the circuit to the summit via the Greenleaf Trail, down the ridge to Little Haystack, then back to the point of origin via the Falling Waters Trail, as beautiful as its name implies. It is a comfortable hut, too, and makes an excellent base for exploring the timberline zones of Franconia and Garfield Ridges.

Geology

The geology of Franconia Ridge is fairly complex. Most of the bedrock in the area consists of intrusions of the White Mountain magma series that formed during the Jurassic period and the earlier intrusions of the New Hampshire series in the late Devonian period. The intrusions of Mt. Lafayette granite porphyry and Mt. Garfield porphyritic quartz syenite (see cross section on pages 26–27) appear to be parts of giant ring dikes. Ring dikes formed by the upwelling of magma along nearly circular fracture zones. The dikes are therefore vertical cylinders with a diameter of 10 to 20 miles and a wall thickness of a mile or less. The cylinders are usually incomplete when viewed from above, but in some locations, such as the Ossipee ring dike in the Ossipee Mountains south of Mt. Chocorua, they may form closed circles.

Throughout the region, evidence of Pleistocene glaciation and post-Pleistocene glacial action may be found. Glacial striations are evident on the exposed bedrock along Franconia Ridge. Although the ravines east of the ridge are primarily stream-cut, there is some evidence of shaping by small valley glaciers.

More details of bedrock geology are given in the section on the walks in the vicinity of Greenleaf Hut.

Ecology

Greenleaf Hut lies in the transition zone between the forest below and the tundra above. As the hut is approached from below, the timber becomes stunted, but is still erect and treelike in form. But at the hut, a dramatic transition occurs. The trees are beginning to take on the form of typical krummholz but are still erect. A few yards away, up the slope toward the summit of Mt. Lafayette, the vegetation becomes prostrate. And not far above that, the trees disappear completely and alpine tundra takes over.

East of the hut and slightly below lie Eagle Lakes with their profusion of bog plants. Sphagnum moss provides a spongy, water-soaked mat that looks deceptively dry—until you step on it. But don't! You'll hurt the plants. Here you can find wren's egg cranberry (*Vaccinium oxycoccus*) with its speckled fruit, the carnivorous sundew (*Drosera rotundifolia*), and three-leaved false Solomon's seal (*Smilacina trifolia*). (True Solomon's seal has pendant flowers dangling from each leaf.) The yellow pond lily is spatter-dock (*Nuphar variegatum*), which usually occurs only at lower elevations.

The pond hosts a colony of spring peepers, the small frog with a loud voice. In 1992, there was at least one beaver in the lake, and snowshoe hares abound in the area.

Greenleaf's bunks are typical of those throughout the hut system. Paul Mozell.

Thus the immediate vicinity of the hut is an excellent place to study the gradations from one ecosystem to another. None of the other huts boasts such a wide variety of habitats and microclimates so close at hand.

A self-guided nature walk at the end of the chapter follows the Greenleaf Trail to the southernmost lake.

Access to the Hut

There are two routes to Greenleaf from the highway: from Lafayette Place Campground via the Old Bridle Path, and from Profile Clearing via the Greenleaf Trail. The Greenleaf Trail is slightly shorter but takes about the same time. The Old Bridle Path is the one used by the hut crews to pack in supplies. It is somewhat more scenic than the Greenleaf Trail and receives considerably heavier use. It also serves as one leg of a very popular circuit over Franconia Ridge that uses the Old Bridle Path and the Falling Waters Trail.

Via Greenleaf Trail. This trail was constructed as a bridle path in the latter part of the last century to replace what is now known as the Old Bridle Path. The trail, blazed in blue, begins at the Cannon Mountain Tramway parking lot on the west side of I-93. From the parking lot, the Greenleaf Trail follows a sidewalk through the parkway underpass, turns left and follows the northbound ramp for 50 yards then turns right across a ditch into the woods (sign). It runs roughly parallel to the parkway, crosses the gravel outwash of a slide and climbs moderately by numerous switchbacks. At about 1.5 miles, the path enters the sharp and spectacular defile of Eagle Pass. Here the path also enters the Lafayette Brook Scenic Area. This was established by the U.S. Forest Service to protect the patches of old-growth timber that occur in the Lafayette Brook drainage. The upper portion of this drainage supports old-growth spruce and balsam fir that is reputed to be virgin timber.

After the level transit of the pass, the trail swings southward and climbs steeply over loose stones, with poor footing in wet weather. It emerges from the trees on the open top of the shoulder it has been climbing and reaches the hut at the junction with the Old Bridle Path.

Trail distance is 2.7 miles and the elevation gain is 2,200 feet. Walking time is 2.5 hours.

Via Old Bridle Path. The Old Bridle Path was apparently constructed around 1840 to service a small hotel on the summit of Mt. Lafayette. At the present time it is the path used by the hut crews at Greenleaf Hut.

The trail begins at a parking lot on the northbound (east) side of I-93, just opposite Lafayette Place Campground. On the southbound side, you can park near the picnic area of the campground and get to the trailhead through a pedestrian tunnel under the highway. An information office on the west side of the highway provides trail and weather information.

The trail heads northeast through a deciduous forest on a moderate grade. You will notice trail sections that have been stabilized by the construction of log "water bars" to carry rainwater off the trail, thereby preventing erosion of the trailbed. Although peeled logs can be very slippery in wet weather, removing the bark retards decay and lengthens the life of the water bars substantially. On steep stretches, log steps are constructed.

On this stretch, the vegetation changes from the lower northern hardwood zone of beech, yellow birch, and sugar maple to the spruce-fir zone dominated by red spruce and balsam fir. A zigzag to the right carries the trail on the contour for a short distance. The trail turns sharply left and continues upward, turning left again to climb the ridge. Proceeding up the ridge over open ledges with fine views, it enters a grove of stunted spruce trees. The steep ascent of the three "Agonies" then begins. These are not so bad with a light pack, but surely deserve their name if one is burdened with 80 pounds of food for the hut. A side path right avoids the steepest part of the Agonies and affords fine views of the steep ravine of Walker Brook. It begins at the top of the first Agony shortly after the loose red rock appears underfoot and rejoins the main path in a few yards. This red rock is a fine-grained granite called aplite. The grains have an almost sugary texture. The red color is from oxidation, or rusting, of minor iron-containing minerals in the rock.

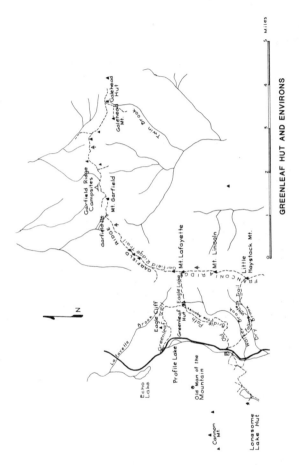

GREENLEAF HUT AND ENVIRONS

At the top of the last Agony, the path levels off for about 200 yards, passing through stunted spruce. The hut appears rather suddenly.

Trail distance is 2.9 miles, and the elevation gain is 2,500 feet. Walking time is 2.5 hours.

Day Hikes from Greenleaf Hut

There are several interesting short walks in the vicinity and one geologically interesting harder walk to the summit of Mt. Lafayette. For an after-dinner stroll, walk 200 feet down the Greenleaf Trail to an unmarked path left that leads to an open rock ledge. This is a favorite place for sunset-watchers.

North Lookout. Just a few yards from the hut is the so-called North Lookout, the only place in the hut system where one hut is visible from the immediate vicinity of another. (Greenleaf and Lonesome Lake huts are both visible from portions of the Greenleaf Trail near the hut.) The view of Franconia Notch and the cliffs of Cannon Mtn. is unsurpassed. Franconia Notch was cut in a V-shape by stream action millions of years ago, but the continental ice sheets of the Pleistocene scoured it into a typical U-shaped glacial trough. The major direction of the ice sheet in this area was from northwest to southeast, but the deep notch diverted a tongue of it southward. As the ice melted, it deposited quantities of glacial drift or till. This irregular mass was generally poorly drained. Where the valley slope was great, subsequent stream action carried much of it downstream. But at the heights-of-land in the notches, ponds remained. In Franconia Notch, one of these ponds— Echo Lake—drains northward into Lafayette Brook while the other—Profile Lake—drains southward into the Pemigewasset River. Many other White Mountain notches have similar ponds at or near the height-of-land.

To the southwest can be seen Lonesome Lake and its hut. Lonesome Lake was also formed by the continental ice sheet.

Mt. Lafayette via the Greenleaf Trail. Apart from the view from the summit of Lafayette, the most interesting feature of the trail to the summit is the opportunity it affords for studying the geology of the Franconia-Lafayette area. Three different igneous rocks are exposed along the route. (See the geological profile on pages 26-27.)

The Greenleaf Trail is underlain by the products of postglacial weathering that have worked their way downslope into the shallow basin. The trail bedrock is Kinsman quartz monzonite for the first few hundred yards. This is a dark, coarse-grained rock containing large phenocrysts of potash feldspar. These large crystals are distinctive and serve to separate it from the other types of bedrock in the area. At the knoll overlooking the lakes and hut, the rock begins to change. Here it is Mt. Lafayette granite porphyry, a lighter gray-green rock also containing crystals of potash feldspar, although the crystals are smaller than those in the monzonite.

Proceeding upward, about halfway to the summit, bedrock changes again, to Mt. Garfield porphyrytic quartz syenite. This rock contains more plagioclase feldspar (containing calcium and sodium as opposed to the potassium in the potash or orthoclase feldspar), giving it a darker color than the Mt. Lafayette granite porphyry. Feldspar crystals are also evident in the syenite. This outcrop is a finger of the ringdike that stretches in an arc from the Franconia Ridge northward and eastward to the Twin Range. It is not seen again until the summit of Garfield is reached.

Near the summit, bedrock changes again to the type exposure of the Mt. Lafayette granite porphyry. The exposure runs north-south along the ridge, to the west of the Garfield syenite dike.

To the north can be seen the dome-shaped summit of the north peak of Lafayette, rounded by glacial action. The boulders lying on the tundra are glacial erratics of meta-morphic rather than igneous origin. They were brought from the metamorphic rock outcrops that occur northwest of Franconia Notch. Glacial striations can also be found on the bedrock exposures.

A few yards southwest of the summit can be found the remains of the foundation of the Lafayette summit house. The roofless walls at the summit provide little protection from the elements today. Lightning storms can be vicious on the unprotected ridges; they are no place to camp during inclement weather. On one July day in 1967, two young boys pitched their tent in the lee of the highest remaining wall. A boiling late afternoon storm crashed lightning near their little tent. Both were injured, but one was able to stumble down the path to the hut, where a mountain rescue was organized. A lull in the storm permitted the rescuers to carry the more seriously injured youth down to the hut. Although burned on every point of contact with the ground (he had been lying on his side), he recovered to hike again. What if the hut and its strong and able crew had not been nearby? The outcome would certainly have been worse.

Trail distance from Greenleaf Hut to the summit of Mt. Lafayette is 1.1 miles with an elevation gain of 1,000 feet. Walking time is 1 hour up and 30 minutes down.

Access to Adjacent Huts

The shortest route to Lonesome Lake Hut is via the Old Bridle Path to Lafayette Place Campground, then via the Lonesome Lake Trail. The route to Galehead Hut follows the arduous Garfield Ridge Trail.

The kitchen of Greenleaf Hut. Paul Mozell.

Lonesome Lake Hut. The Old Bridle Path leads south from the hut. It is nearly level for few hundred yards, then descends the Agonies rather steeply. It finally swings left off the ridge toward Walker Brook, then bends right, contouring away from the brook. After 125 yards, the trail bends sharply left and heads downward. It reaches I-93 opposite Lafayette Place Campground. Hikers should use the pedestrian tunnel under the highway.

The Lonesome Lake Trail is described on page 63. Trail distance is 4.3 miles, and the elevation gain is 900 feet. Walking time is 3.5 hours.

Galehead Hut. The Garfield Ridge Trail has the reputation for being the most tiring trail in the White Mountains. The ridge is full of little bumps, many of which are not shown on the trail maps, and the trail goes over every one of them. Indeed, sometimes the trail seems to go up and down even where there is no bump present. Although the Pleistocene glaciers have been blamed for the difficulty of the trail, without the glaciers the ridge probably would have been more rugged. The continental ice sheet did a good job of rounding off the craggy spires of the ridge.

But there are rewards for the ridge runner. The first part of the route is above timberline, with fine views of the Pemigewasset Wilderness. There are good views from the bare summit of Garfield, and the trail has a wilderness character that helps make the journey less tiresome.

The route climbs the cone of Mt. Lafayette on the Greenleaf Trail (see page 81 for detailed description of this portion of the trail). From the summit, the Garfield Ridge Trail leads over open slopes to the north summit. It then descends the northeast ridge. A quarter-mile below the north summit, the Skookumchuck Trail diverges left. The trail continues its descent past interesting rock formations. Here bedrock changes from the Mt. Lafayette granite porphyry back to Kinsman quartz monzonite, the same as at the hut.

After proceeding over a large hump, the trail descends to a wooded col and then starts the long climb to Mt. Garfield. In a short distance, the trail passes to the south (right) of Garfield Pond and starts to ascend the summit of Garfield. The trail does not cross the summit but reaches its highest point about 60 yards north. The summit is bare and is easily reached from this point; the views are worth the detour. Two hundred yards beyond this point, a junction is reached: the Garfield Trail leads straight ahead to Route 3 while the Garfield Ridge Trail turns right and descends the steep east side of the summit. Beyond the steep part, a side trail leads left for the Garfield Ridge Campsite. There are tent platforms and a shelter at the campsite (fee charged), supervised by a resident caretaker.

The main trail crosses a brook and drops down into a col where the Franconia Brook Trail branches right. Beyond this junction, the trail climbs up and down a number of minor bumps on the ridge, finally meeting the Gale River Trail, which enters from the left. From this junction, the trail slabs up the north side of Galehead Mtn. on a moderate grade, then turns right and climbs to a junction with the Twinway and the Frost Trail 40 yards from Galehead Hut. Turn right to reach the hut.

Trail distance is 7.5 miles and the total elevation gain is about 2,700 feet. Walking time is 6 hours.

▼ ▼ ▼

A Self-Guided Nature Walk
Greenleaf Hut
by Ray Welch

To start your walk, go out the main entrance of the hut on the southeast side and stand on the wooden deck, looking east toward Mt. Lafayette. This is Station One.

Station One

You are standing at an elevation a bit over 4,000 feet. If the weather is clear, you are looking up at the summit of Mt. Lafayette, a little under a mile away and 5,249 feet high. Lafayette is the tallest peak in the western White Mountains, although Mt. Washington is more than 1,000 feet higher. Even so, the summit—and the ridge from Lafayette to Little Haystack—is tall enough to provide the climatic conditions that support the treeless, arctic-like community called tundra. The hut is right at the transition

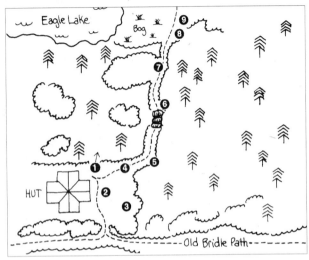

between tundra and the boreal forest, dominated by balsam fir. You can see the stunted, stressed look to the nearby trees, which here are near their limits of climatic tolerance. The climate was even worse in the past; the glaciers of the ice age left this spot not much more than 10,000 years ago. The mountain has been here much longer but has been "Mt. Lafayette" only since being named for this Revolutionary War hero in the early nineteenth century.

Station Two

Walk down the steps and look at the surrounding bedrock and at the foundation of the hut, largely made of the same rock. This is an igneous rock, which, laid down in a melted state deep in the Earth, cooled and solidified about 200 million years ago. This event was part of the dramatic goings-on when the supercontinent Pangea began to split, creating the present-day Atlantic Ocean. This now-exposed rock relic of that era is a form of granite called

Kinsman quartz monzonite, one of the most striking rocks in New Hampshire. The white, rectangular spots are crystals of feldspar, a potassium-rich mineral that weathers into clays. Across Franconia Notch is Cannon Mtn. (and the Old Man), whose cliffs are a different type of granite, Conway granite, pinkish and without these large crystals. Keep your eyes open to the rock types as you hike in this area and you will see such differences.

Station Three

Go back toward the water-storage tanks behind the hut to the slight rock rise below them. As you go, look at the ground around you. Heavy foot traffic over the years has nearly wiped out the natural vegetation on this spot, and only a few hardy species manage to hang on—mostly where a crevice or sheltering rock keeps feet off the plant. There is some moss, common everywhere in the mountains; a grass species or two; and most noticeably, with its light green color, tufts of small leaves, and (for much of the summer) white, five-petaled flowers, the mountain sandwort. This is an arctic-alpine plant whose preference for a barren, sandy soil, along with its rapid growth (it's a chickweed relative) allows it to succeed on this disturbed spot. Most tundra vegetation is nowhere near so tolerant of foot traffic, so no other tundra plants flourish here. As you hike, think of this, and keep your feet on the trail.

Station Four

Go to where the Greenleaf Trail heads toward Mt. Lafayette. Stop just where it enters the low scrub at the edge of the hut clearing. You can see clearly that the evergreens here show the stress mentioned at Station One—

there are branches with dead needles and branches with no needles at all. These dead and dying parts all over the balsam fir trees reveal the effects of many stresses: flying and abrasive snow in winter, drying winds in summer and winter, heat stress, cold stress, and mechanical damage from the buildup of frozen fog (rime ice). When you proceed to further stations downslope you will see that a bit of shelter below the brow of the hill lets the firs get bigger. But as you rise up beyond Eagle Lakes, the trees quickly dwindle to their final form, dwarfed and stunted, called krummholz. Eventually they give up entirely and yield the mountain to the pure tundra plants beyond.

Station Five

A few feet farther on, the trail makes a sharp left turn and begins to descend. There is a square rock in the trail at this spot. Stop there. You are in a lichen paradise. The fogs that sweep these slopes (clouds, actually) and can freeze to form the damaging rime ice covering the firs, also help provide one condition that lichens need: moisture. Rain, fog-drip, and melted ice and snow often saturate the ground. On the left, under trees, are pale clumps and cups of reindeer lichen and cup lichen, along with darker horn lichen. On the right, the trunks of both dead and living firs are covered with the gray sheets and layers of other lichen species; even dead twigs have clusters of lichen on them. These curious organisms (a fungus/alga symbiosis) are plantlike in that they need light, carbon dioxide, and water to grow. Light and carbon dioxide are no problem, but, lacking roots, lichens must depend on the direct uptake of water from their surfaces—though the supply is hardly a problem in our soppy mountains.

Station Six

Begin your descent; about 40 feet farther on, the trail comes to some big, blocky steps down. Stop at the top of these. Again, look at the edges of the trail. As before, there is a different microclimate near the ground. Here there is protection from the worst of the winds, moisture from fog-drip and rain, and light without shading trees. These all combine to produce lush growths of one of our most common plants—moss. Nearly the most primitive of all plants, it is, like lichens, hardy and widespread. Here there are tight pale green or green-red mounds of sphagnum moss and the darker, loosely arranged leaves of star moss. In this area you can also see the shamrocklike leaves of mountain sorrel, and perhaps its flowers. Look as you will, however, you will never see moss flowers—like ferns, another simple plant, moss is nonflowering.

Station Seven

Go down the trail about 100 feet more. On your left, you will see an irregular clearing in the trees. This opening is not natural but is the result of past camping activity and cutting of wood for fires. Although the plants and animals of the mountains here can withstand rigorous conditions, the balance between disturbance and regeneration is precarious. Many disturbances can so disrupt a community that they take far longer to recover than ones at lowland locations. Even though this spot has been left alone for many years now, and has a rich growth of wood aster, skunk currant, grasses, rushes, and ferns, there are only the slightest signs that the trees are coming back—a few fir seedlings. Given enough time, however, the site should support trees again—although this return will be a problem for the asters, currants, grasses, and sedges.

Station Eight

Descend the rest of the hill to the low point before the trail begins to climb again. Stop. To your left, the ground is marshy, and beyond you can see some of Eagle Lake. There are no eagles here, and the lake is ever so slowly on its way out. The lake-erasing is well begun, and the low, wet area between you and the lake is a bog, evidence of the process of ecological succession that gradually turns shallow ponds into plant-, peat-, and sediment-choked basins, shifting them from the aquatic to the terrestrial. Close to you the grasslike plant is beaked sedge, rather uncommon in the mountains. Beyond is sphagnum moss and other bog plants. In time—centuries to a few thousand years—nothing might clearly mark the former lake, and fir and spruce will grow where yellow pond lilies now dot the water.

Station Nine

On Thursday, July 15, 1858, Henry David Thoreau passed by this spot on his way up Mt. Lafayette and collected dead twigs to build a fire "on the moss and lichens, by a rock amid the shallow fir," and boil water for tea. He saw the yellow pond lilies you see today and the bog and its vegetation, noting that "the outlet of the pond was considerable; but soon lost beneath the rocks." You, too, can climb on from here as far as you wish, even to the summit, and all around you the mountain is much the same as it was a century ago and will continue to be so for a long time to come.

7
Galehead Hut

From the Hut Log: September 20, 1938 [The devastating 1938 hurricane hit New England on September 21.]

> Arrived about 5 p.m. from Greenleaf hut—fog and heavy rain after leaving Mt. Lafayette. September 21
>
> Rain and high wind, fog. Plan to start for Zealand Falls Hut tomorrow *if* weather improves. Roof leaks in wood box and on stove—moved it.
>
> **William A. Balch, Montclair, NJ**

G ALEHEAD is the most isolated of all the huts. It sits on a little bump on Garfield Ridge and commands a view of the vast expanse of the Pemigewasset Wilderness (the Pemi is a federally designated wilderness area). Mountains and valleys stretch southward in unbroken waves of green. Viewing the placid expanse of forest on a calm summer day, it is difficult to imagine what it was like barely a hundred years ago. Then the silence was broken by the puffing of logging engines and the creak of flatcars hauling their loads of logs down to the mills at Lincoln. The rasp of crosscut saws and the crash of falling timber startled the inhabitants of the primeval spruce forest.

It was not always so. Only a few years before, the Pemi was indeed an untracked wilderness. Sweetser's *The White Mountains* for 1890 (based on information gathered as late as 1888) describes it this way:

Galehead Hut. Lou Lainey.

The term Pemigewasset has been applied to the great wilderness which surrounds the East Branch and its tributaries....This broad region is still in a condition of primeval wildness, and has not yet been invaded by clearings, roads, or trails. Clear to Franconia Notch extends this untracked and unvisited realm of Nature, who yet holds one fastness in the heart of busy New England, with its glorious falls not yet harnessed as "water powers", and its stately trees yet undeveloped into sashes and blinds....This inner solitude should be entered only under the guidance of experienced foresters; and travelling will be found very slow and arduous. The scenery is simply that of a vast primeval forest, most of the environing mountains being hidden by the foliage or by intervening ridges.

Apparently Sweetser did not know that logging was already proceeding southward in the then New Zealand Valley and by 1887 had reached Shoal Pond. Indeed, Zealand Valley is not mentioned in Sweetser's guide. (The origin of the name is lost to history, but the valley was probably reminiscent of New Zealand in its remoteness.) The lumbermen were also on their way from the west. In a few years they had pushed their logging railroads up the East Branch of the Pemigewasset River from Lincoln. They "cut out" and "got out," abandoning the land to unchecked fire and eventually to the restorative powers of nature.

And so today, although the forest is no longer primeval, it is unbroken and appears to anyone scanning the forest from the promontory near Galehead Hut much as it must have appeared to the intrepid visitor of 125 years ago. To the ecologist and historian there is, of course, abundant evidence of the occupation and devastation of the Pemi. But to the casual hiker intent on seeking the solitude of wilderness, it is wilderness enough.

The hut that overlooks this peaceful scene was built in 1931. It and Zealand Falls were conceived as the completing links in the chain of huts from Lonesome Lake on the west to Carter Notch on the east. The hut was built of the trees that covered the site. Magnificent conifers, spared by the loggers who had cleared the slopes below, provided both the materials from which the walls were made and an overspreading shade. But the shade did not last long. On September 21, 1938, a giant hurricane roared northward across the Connecticut coast and slashed its way up the spine of New England. Unlike most hurricanes, which lose their strength as they move over land, this one retained much of its intensity. The Mt. Washington Observatory recorded sustained winds of 136 miles per hour.

The trees of the exposed ridges were no match. Devastation was extensive. The fine stand of timber surrounding Galehead Hut was gone, now a jackstraw tangle of downed stems. Although a half-century of decay has reduced them to piles of brown organic dust, the outlines of many are traced by mats of covering moss. New trees are growing up, obscuring the view that was opened up by the great wind.

Galehead Hut was patterned after Greenleaf, built two years earlier. The floor plan today is the same as when it was built: kitchen and common room end-to-end, with bunkrooms on either side forming a stubby cross. There are accommodations for 36. The hut is normally operated by a crew of four and is open for full service from early June to early September. A caretaker is present for the month preceding and the month following the regular summer season.

Geology

The geological history of Garfield Ridge is rather complicated. It is a story of long periods of volcanic activity during which bodies of molten rock pushed into the crust, forming dikes of granite. Blocks of heavy rocks sank into the magma. As the masses cooled, great fractures developed, permitting the intrusion of yet other masses of magma. Subsequent eons of erosion dissected the landscape in patterns that are little related to the bedrock, for much of it is more or less equally resistant to erosion. The features that exist today are the result of stream erosion modified to a small degree by the workings of continental glaciation.

The bedrock in the immediate vicinity of the hut is Mt. Lafayette granite porphyry, a hard, massive gray or green rock. It contains phenocrysts of various sorts: hexagonal quartz crystals, white feldspar crystals, and tiny black crystals of various composition. The rock mass itself is fine grained and composed of essentially the same minerals that compose the phenocrysts. It is older than the Mt.

Garfield quartz syenite that underlies the north and west slopes of Mt. Garfield.

There is some evidence of valley glaciation in the vicinity. The ravines on the sides of the Mt. Bond–Twin Mtn. ridge are poorly developed cirques. Evidence of continental glaciation can also be found. The asymmetrical form of Galehead Mtn. as seen from the hut resulted from the grinding action of a continental glacier as it pushed its way over the summit from the northwest. The southeast face steepened as the ice plucked blocks from the summit.

Ecology

The progress of revegetation after the severe jolt that the 1938 hurricane dealt to the forest ecosystem can be seen right around the hut. After every disruption, the forces of nature work to reestablish the vegetation. What comes back is usually not what was there before; some earlier stage in ecological succession usually asserts itself. But in the New England mountains, unless the surface has been bared to bedrock, vegetation comes back quickly. Indeed, it is difficult to prevent trees from reclaiming a disturbed area.

A good example of this can be seen in the diagonal green strips that slant up many of the ridges in the Pemigewasset Wilderness. Years ago, the loggers created skid roads down which they hauled the logs to the railroad in the valley below. These bare strips of earth created a perfect seedbed for the light-seeded birch. So the birches quickly invaded the old roads creating long strips of vegetation that are lighter in color than the adjoining mixed hardwoods.

The gray patches that can be seen throughout the Pemi are of a different origin. These patches started as openings in the forest, perhaps where the wind blew down a group of old trees, perhaps where a fire created a small opening in the canopy. Whatever the cause, an opening in the forest was created. But this opening has one side exposed to the wind and one side protected. New trees can grow on the protected side, but the trees on the exposed side are subject to the fierceness of the winter winds. Weaker trees are killed, enlarging the opening, which in turn allows more wind to work havoc. So the opening grows downwind and at the same time is filled in by new growth upwind. The result is an opening that proceeds slowly (perhaps a foot or two a year) in the direction of the destructive winds. From a distance, these parallel openings appear as ripples on the slope; they are appropriately known as fir waves.

For more on the ecology of the area, see the self-guided nature walk at the end of this chapter.

Access to the Hut

There is only one way in to Galehead that does not involve an initial climb over a mountain or a long 10-mile walk through the heart of the Pemigewasset Wilderness. The route usually taken starts from U.S. Route 3 and proceeds up the north branch of the Gale River.

Via Gale River Trail. The Gale River Loop Road (FR 92) to the trailhead leaves Route 3 at "Five Corners" (Trudeau Road), a road junction 0.3 mile east of the bridge that spans Gale River. At 0.65 mile south of the intersection, bear left (the right-hand fork leads to Littleton Reservoir). The road turns right and crosses the North Branch and at 1.65 miles from Route 3 reaches the trailhead and parking lot on the left.

The Gale River Trail starts on a gentle grade through the hardwood forest, crosses a tributary of the North

Branch, then crosses over a low ridge to the main stream. At 1.75 miles from the trailhead, it recrosses to the east side and follows quite close to the river. The trail then crosses back to the west side and follows an old logging road on a gentle grade. After traversing the bases of two slides, the trail bears right away from the stream and starts to climb on a steeper grade. In 0.5 mile, it joins the Garfield Ridge Trail, which it follows left to Galehead Hut.

Trail distance is 4.2 miles and the elevation gain is 2,200 feet. Walking time is about 3 hours.

Day Hikes from Galehead Hut

Most of those who stay at Galehead are on their way somewhere else. It is not a destination point for very many. Nevertheless there are many interesting things to be seen in the immediate vicinity. The views into the Pemigewasset Wilderness from the hut and from lookout points along Garfield Ridge are many and varied. There are long stretches of dwarf boreal forest along the ridge and patches of krummholz along the ridge between Mt. Guyot and South Twin.

Galehead Mtn. via Frost Trail. The asymmetrical summit of Galehead has already been commented on. The summit is easily reached via the Frost Trail, which leads south from the hut. In about 300 yards, the Twin Brook Trail to Franconia Brook leaves left. The Frost Trail then climbs on a moderate grade to the summit. The views of the Pemi to the south and Franconia Ridge to the west are excellent.

Round trip distance is 1 mile and the elevation gain is 200 feet. Walking time to the top is about 25 minutes.

South Twin via the Twinway. When the 1967 topographic map was issued by the U.S. Geological Survey,

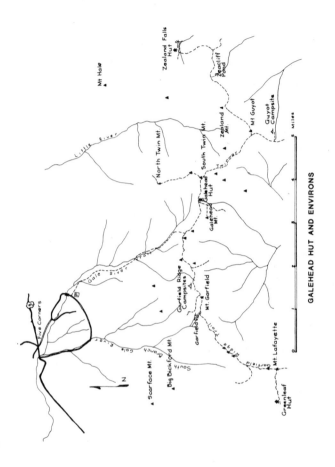

GALEHEAD HUT AND ENVIRONS

South Twin lost 24 feet of elevation (most likely due to a surveyor's error, since nothing has come along to lop off the top of the mountain). It is now officially 4,902 feet high, but it is still the eighth-highest mountain in New Hampshire. The lowered official elevation doesn't make the steep climb to the summit seem any less exhausting. It is less than a mile but will take more than an hour.

The Twinway, part of the Appalachian Trail and blazed in white, drops down from the hut for a few feet, then climbs straight up the western ridge. The climb is steep and rocky. Just below the summit, the Twinway branches right. The last 50 feet to the summit follow the North Twin Spur.

Because of its height, there are fine views in all directions. The top is ledgy and mostly bare. The ledges show glacial striations from the continental ice sheet. In common with the entire route from the hut to Zeacliff, the summit bedrock is Mt. Lafayette granite porphyry. Phenocrysts of white quartz are embedded in the gray rock. The bedrock is very uniform along the Twinway; specimens from Zealand Mtn. are similar to those on South Twin.

The vegetation on the top is scrubby with patches of krummholz, typical of the White Mountain vegetation just at timberline.

Trail distance to the summit is 0.8 mile and the elevation gain is 1,100 feet. Scrambling time is just over an hour up, 45 minutes down.

Access to Adjacent Huts

Galehead Hut is almost exactly halfway between Greenleaf and Zealand Falls huts. Greenleaf is 7.5 miles to the west, Zealand is 7 miles to the east. In either direction, the walk is moderately arduous, but richly endowed with fine views. Both routes stay on the ridgetops and traverse the peaks. Much of the way is through scrub and over ledges so that lookout points are numerous.

Twinway to Zealand Falls Hut. This trail, part of the Appalachian Trail and blazed with white paint, traverses three 4,000-foot peaks—Zealand, Guyot, and South Twin—and passes within a mile of three others: Mt. Bond, West Bond, and North Twin. It comes close to timberline and much of the way is through stunted krummholz. There are many fine views of the mountains surrounding the Pemigewasset Wilderness.

From the hut, the Twinway leads northeastward on a slight drop, then turns eastward and starts straight up the west ridge of South Twin. The trail climbs rapidly over ledges and a certain amount of scrambling is necessary. Near the summit, a junction is reached: the North Twin Spur leads to the summit of South Twin in 50 feet (and the top of North Twin [4,761 feet] in 1.25 miles); the Twinway continues southward. The Twinway slabs downward through scrubby trees, then crosses the broad, flat saddle between South Twin and Guyot. The trail than climbs moderately through the krummholz, meets the Bondcliff Trail to Mt. Bond (4,698 feet, 1.25 miles south) and turns left for the summit of Mt. Guyot (4,580 feet). The views from this part of the trail are superb on a clear day. But it is exposed and is often cold and windy.

The Twinway drops rapidly down the northeast ridge of Guyot to the Guyot-Zealand col, then climbs the wooded summit of Zealand Mtn. The summit is a few yards north of the trail on a short spur marked by a cairn. There are no views, but it is one of the official 4,000-footers. Continuing along the ridge, the trail goes over a number of minor bumps before reaching the cliffs overlooking Zeacliff Pond. It descends 200 feet to a col where a trail branches right to the pond and an unreliable spring.

In 0.5 mile the Zeacliff Trail joins from the right. In a few yards, a loop trail leads right to a viewpoint overlooking Zealand Notch and the vast expanse of the Pemigewasset Wilderness. The view from here is unsurpassed. Don't miss it. The loop trail continues northward over the ledges and quickly rejoins the Twinway. From the junction, the Twinway drops rapidly through a beautiful forest of spruce alternating with white birch. A short distance after crossing Whitewall Brook, the Lend-a-Hand Trail joins from the left; the Twinway turns right and follows the brook 0.3 mile to the hut.

Total trail distance is 7 miles and the elevation gain is about 1,700 feet, two-thirds of which is gained in the initial climb to the summit of South Twin. Walking time is 4.5 hours.

Garfield Ridge Trail to Greenleaf Hut. The trail along the ridge has a well-deserved reputation for being one of the most arduous in the region. The footway is rough and goes over innumerable bumps along the ridge. It always seems to take longer than planned. But there are rewards: the views from Garfield are exceptional. And in good weather the walk over the barren north ridge of Mt. Lafayette is a delight.

From its junction with the Twinway and the Frost Trail, 40 yards from the hut, the Garfield Ridge Trail leads first north, then quickly swings northwestward, slabbing diagonally down the north slope of Galehead Mtn. In about 0.5 mile, near a low point, the Gale River Trail enters right. The trail climbs around the north side of a minor summit, then goes up and down several times before meeting the Franconia Brook Trail in a col. Water is found here. Shortly after climbing out of the col, the side trail to

Garfield Ridge Campsite is reached. There is a shelter here, plus seven tent platforms, all in the charge of a caretaker. A fee is charged for overnight use.

From the campsite, the trail climbs steeply toward the summit of Mt. Garfield (4,500 feet). The Garfield Trail north to Route 3 branches right a short distance below the summit. Soon the bare summit of Garfield is reached. The nature of the bedrock changes near the summit. Garfield is underlain by Mt. Garfield porphyritic quartz syenite; on either side, the bedrock is Kinsman quartz monzonite. The syenite is similar to granite but without as much quartz; both are igneous rocks formed by the cooling of magma. The Mt. Garfield rock contains orthoclase feldspar (potassium aluminum silicate) that weathers easily, producing a rotten rock. The Kinsman quartz monzonite is finer grained and contains a larger mixture of plagioclase feldspar composed of calcium and sodium silicates. It is a less erodible rock than the syenite.

Beyond the summit, the trail drops westward to Garfield Pond, which it passes near the south shore. It then swings southwest and starts the long climb along Garfield Ridge. After numerous ups and downs (more ups than downs), the trail reaches timberline at about 4,500 feet. Soon the Skookumchuck Trail leaves right for Route 3. It then climbs to the north summit of Mt. Lafayette and continues the gentle climb along the open ridge to the main summit. The bedrock here is Mt. Lafayette granite porphyry, a coarse-grained rock containing phenocrysts of orthoclase feldspar. The crystals are nearly round and are set in a dark gray-green groundmass.

From the summit, the trail (now the Greenleaf Trail), descends past the ruins of the foundation of the old summit house, then along the western ridge. From points on the ridge, both Greenleaf Hut and Lonesome Lake Hut—at the south shore of the pond visible high above Franconia Notch to the southwest—can be seen. The trail drops into the scrub above Eagle Lakes, two shallow glacial tarns, which it passes to the left. After a short climb, the trail emerges from the scrub at the hut.

Total trail distance is 7.6 miles and the elevation gain is about 3,300 feet. Walking time is 5.5 hours.

▼ ▼ ▼

Self-Guided Nature Walk
Galehead Hut
by Ray Welch

To start your walk, go back down the short side trail to the hut to its intersection with the Appalachian Trail. Stop here. This is Station One.

Station One

Welcome to Canada—or at least, welcome to a Canadian forest zone. Here at 3,800 feet, the mountain's elevation has lifted you from the warmer climate of the valley, with its northern hardwood forest full of beech, maple, and birch, into this boreal forest, full of more northerly species such as spruce and balsam fir. Climatic telescoping is extreme in the White Mountains. A climb to the top of Mt. Lafayette or Mt. Washington takes you to the equivalent of the Arctic, where even trees fall away, and you enter the open land called tundra. Even here, somewhat lower, you are in a rigorous climate, and the forest is slow growing

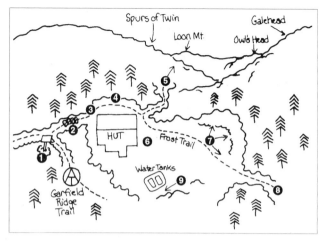

and fragile. Notice how small the trees are. Yet they are 40 years old or more. See how erosion has cut the soil away along the trail back toward the hut. This slash in the woods lets in light and provides an opportunity for other species; the pale-leafed shrub behind the sign is mountain holly, the deciduous tree behind that is a paper birch, and the trail-side green fringe is sphagnum moss. Think "Cool, damp, and Canada," and you are on your way.

Station Two

Go toward the hut and stop by the front of the first porch. Near the open and well-lighted foundation are plants not found in the woods. The hut was built in the 1930s and the site has been much visited, and so continually disturbed, since then. The low grasses on either side of the bare foot-path are actually lawn grass, planted some time ago to help stabilize the soil. Where a lawn is found, weeds often appear, too. You can spot several lowland types here, but most noticeable, right up against the porch base, is one with three-parted, strawberrylike leaves. It's not a straw-berry but instead a common weed called rough cinquefoil. Weeds are opportunists and take advantage of disturbed spots. They grow rapidly but cannot maintain themselves in a mature and developed community like the woods a lit-tle bit beyond you. Your presence, and the hut maintained for you, create a perpetual disturbance and make this a weed haven—we will see more later.

Station Three

In front of the hut's dining room window, nailed to a tree, is a Frost Trail sign. Go over and look closely, not at the sign but at the tree (a balsam fir). The trunk is covered with crusty, gray-green patches of what look like disease or rot. But the tree is not sick. These growths are harmless lichens, an odd organism consisting of a fungus and an alga inter-grown and mutually dependent in a symbiosis. Lichen species are everywhere on these mountains: on rocks, on the ground, and on tree bark. Like plants, they live on water; minerals dissolved in fog, rain, or snowmelt (precip-itation is anything but 100 percent "pure" water); and sun-light. Although they grow slowly and don't look plantlike, they are not parasites. They share traits with the more tradi-tional plants under the trees: the narrow-leafed, sharp-toothed wood aster, and the shamrocklike mountain sorrel. There are dozens of species of local lichens. Learning one from the other is a long task, but the one on the branches is puffed shield lichen, common everywhere in these woods.

Station Four

Beyond the second porch of the hut, a side trail bears left on a short descent to an overlook. Stop when you can go no farther. The ground drops abruptly away and (weather permitting) gives you a splendid view of wilderness. Although it seems entirely wild at first glance, a closer looks show signs of human disturbance. On the distant ridge that straddles the valley between Mt. Garfield and South Twin, two slashes cut into the trees. These are ski trails at Loon Mountain and seem a defacement of the nearer Pemigewasset Wilderness. Yet signs of a far greater disturbance about a hundred years ago also are here to see. If you look to the left of the valley bottom at the great descending ridge from South Twin, halfway up are two or three light-green lines cutting more or less horizontally through the trees. These are the signs of old logging roads, relics of the lumbering of these forests. The abandoned roads provided a perfect seedbed for pure birch stands, and these contrast with the mixed birch and conifer woods alongside. The woods have healed themselves, but this is not a virgin wilderness. Natural scars are the talus fields near the ridge-top above, piles of shattered, unstable rock that 10,000 years have been unable to clothe with vegetation.

Station Five

Go back up the trail to the near corner of the porch and look into the clearing beyond, toward Galehead. Near the hut are three balsam firs; all now healthy adolescents, having been protected as seedlings by sprouting next to a sheltering rock. Go to the nearest one. The bedrock of the area around you is exposed. It is a nondescript grayish rock called Kinsman granite porphyry (or Kinsman quartz monzonite), but the rock at the base of this tree looks different, with a coarsely splotched pattern of whitish grays. The dull white material is crystals of feldspar; the shiny gray one is quartz. The rock is not a piece of the bedrock, nor is the large pink boulder the water tanks perch on. These are both clear evidence of great disturbance—the glaciers of the Pleistocene, the great ice age, melted and left behind their final loads of rocky debris, picked up from other spots far off. These noticeable erratics are tombstones that mark the grave of the ice age.

Station Six

Walk across the clearing to where there is a slight drop-off, like the edge of a rock terrace. Look up and you see Galehead Mtn. nearby and Mt. Garfield farther off to the right. Both are examples of the same event that brought the glacial erratics to this clearing. The right-hand slope of each is more gradual than the one to the left. The ice sheets moved right to left from your perspective, sliding upslope smoothly, but roughly plucking at the rock after going over the top, steepening that side. Look down at your feet, and you can likely see evidence of a very recent disturbance—the grazing of plants by animals. The rounded pellets that may lie in little heaps among the short, meadowy plants are from snowshoe hares, who enjoy the rich and tender growth of such things as grasses, chickweed, and dandelion. Come back at dusk and look for them. But if you listen now you might hear some of the birds that live around the hut: winter wrens, with their jumbled, liquid whistles; boreal chickadees; and yellow-rumped warblers.

Station Seven

Take the Frost Trail out of the clearing and toward Galehead. Just before you go into the thick growth of firs, look again at the open ground on either side of the trail. The vegetation is nondescript and not overlush, but it is on the ground and covers it fairly well. Once you enter the woods, this disappears suddenly as if cleared deliberately away. You are seeing the effects of microhabitat variation. The trees produce dense shade and a heavy "rain" of shed needles. Unadapted to the dim light and the smothering mulch, the clearing plants give way to an almost barren ground where only a few wood ferns and a tuft of mountain sorrel make their homes. As you go through the mountains, these shifts from one sort of community to another reflect the nature of all habitats, where life is a constant struggle for survival. If some essential need is unmet or insufficient, a species will vanish, yet these conditions can provide an opportunity for other species. The process by which plants colonize a disturbed habitat and then are replaced by others as the habitat shifts back to its undisturbed make-up is called ecological succession.

Station Eight

Return to the hut clearing and stand on the highest point of bedrock just this side of the water-tank boulder. If you look to the left of the water tanks, to the distant ridge, you see irregular ranks of dead trees, fir waves, which are not storm damage but a slow cycle of die-off and renewal that moves across a slope in about a 75-year period, a human lifetime. Among the waves are scars more suddenly incised down the landscape—avalanches. These raw streaks, formed in seconds, take decades to heal. Most change in these woods is more subtle: a tree falls, a trail is cut, the climate shifts slightly. No wilderness—no community—is really static and changeless, and an almost imperceptible pulse of disturbance and response operates endlessly.

8
Zealand Falls Hut

From the Hut Log: July 30, 1947

> The hut with the most wonderful view in the system.
> **Bonnie Goodwin, Pittsfield, MA**

ONE visitor to the Zealand Valley in 1892 was appalled by what he saw. He recorded his impressions in an editorial in the *Boston Transcript* of Wednesday, July 20:

> The beautiful Zealand Valley is one vast scene of waste and desolation; immense heaps of sawdust roll down the slopes to choke the stream and, by the destructive acids distilled from their decaying substance, to poison the fish; smoke rises night and day from fires which are maintained to destroy the still accumulating piles of slabs and other mill debris.

Today, the hiker viewing the valley from the front porch of Zealand Falls Hut finds it difficult to believe that it is the same valley. The scene is once again that of a pristine wilderness. Unbroken forest stretches southward to Carrigain Notch and Mt. Carrigain itself. Only a few clues betray the early history of the area: the horizontal stripe across the valley at the foot of Whitewall is the trace of an abandoned logging railroad; the bare rock on Whitewall resulted from the fires that so disturbed the *Transcript* editorial writer. Nature's great restorative powers have eliminated most of the traces of the earlier destruction, though a few still remain.

Zealand Falls Hut. Jerry Shereda.

Zealand Notch provides the easiest access from the north to the vast Pemigewasset Wilderness. Zealand Pond, curiously at the highest point of the notch, lies at an elevation of 2,500 feet, less than 1,000 feet above Zealand Campground on Route 302 and only 200 feet above the start of the summer trail at the end of Zealand Road. The hut itself sits on a small ledge about 200 feet higher than the pond, on the west side of the notch. It is immediately adjacent to Whitewall Brook and just above Zealand Falls, a series of cascades along this steep flank of the valley.

The original hut was built in 1932, one of the last two links in the chain connecting the western huts with those in the Presidentials. Building materials were brought up by the old logging railroad grade from Zealand Campground, partly by tractor, partly by burro. The building had been completely framed at a mill yard in Vermont, the lumber labeled and the structure dismantled for transport to the roadhead. The tractor then hauled the precut pieces halfway up the trail, where the burros took over. Despite one of the rainiest Junes on record, 40 tons of material were hauled to the building site by the end of the month. The hut was essentially completed by the end of August, but was not opened to hikers until the next summer. In 1990 the crew quarters and kitchen were enlarged and improved.

Logging in the Zealand Valley

The year 1880 marks the beginning of a cycle of forest destruction and rebirth that is still going on today. It was in that year that J. E. Henry made his first purchase of land in the Zealand Valley area. Until that time the great basin of the East Branch of the Pemigewasset had lain almost unvisited by whites. Samuel C. Eastman's *The White Mountain Guide Book,* 1869 edition, makes no mention of the region; and Moses F. Sweetser's guidebook of 1890 says little more, except to caution that "the inner solitudes should be entered only under the guidance of experienced foresters and traveling will be found very slow and arduous." According to John T. B. Mudge in *The White Mountains* (1992), the origin of the name Zealand Valley has been lost. It may be a reference to New Zealand because of the region's remoteness.

Henry may not have been an experienced forester, but he knew a good tract of marketable timber when he saw one, and in 1881 he began logging operations in the lower reaches of the Zealand River. That year also marked the beginning of the short-lived village of Zealand near the site of today's campground.

Construction of the railroad line up the Zealand River started in 1884 and was completed through the notch as far as Shoal Pond by 1887, a distance of 10 miles. Henry logged as he built, and produced the devastation that so distressed the *Transcript* editorial writer. No thought was given to the future of the forest. It was not until some years later that the U.S. Forest Service was established and the first forestry school started in the United States.

But logging of the sort practiced by J. E. Henry and his sons leaves behind great quantities of debris: treetops and branches, trees too small or too poor to warrant hauling to the mill, and dead snags. Today the forests of the White Mountains are often referred to as "asbestos" forests. But logging debris, dead and drying, will burn, and burn it did. The first recorded fire in the area occurred in 1886; it burned not only the logged area but also the virgin spruce and reportedly consumed 12,000 acres, nearly 20 square miles of the Zealand drainage. In 1903, Zealand burned again, ravaging an extensive area of 10,000 acres. The fire burned through much of the area burned in the 1886 fire. Henry's loggers had left by this time, but the debris remained.

The "cut-out and get-out" logging and vast, intense fires marked these years. Would anything ever grow here again? In many places, the shallow litter covering the bedrock was entirely consumed. Later rains washed the ashes away, leading to slides and exposed rock, now plainly visible in the bare patches of Whitewall. But in other places, the process of revegetation began almost immediately after the fires.

Today the Zealand area is an excellent place to see the processes of postfire succession. Immediately after the fires, pin cherry and red maple seeds that had escaped the intense heat of the fires germinated quickly. Other shrubby species sprang up to help clothe the denuded wasteland. Gradually, larger hardwoods such as beech, yellow and white birch, and maple replaced the low growth. Much of the area is now covered with a beech-birch-maple hardwood forest, but red spruce and balsam fir are gradually mixing in. These more tolerant trees will ultimately replace much of the hardwood forest. Eventually, the forest will look much as it did before the logging and burning.

Geology

Zealand Notch displays the typical U-shape of a glacier-worn valley. The great ice sheets of the late Pleistocene ground their way through the notch, which at one time had the V-shape of a stream-eroded valley. Carrigain Notch, another U-shaped, glacier-worn valley, is visible from the hut, though one has to climb the Zeacliff Trail some distance in order to see the bottom of the notch.

Bedrock in Zealand Notch is Conway granite, an igneous rock that was formed some 150 million years ago.

The Pemigewasset Wilderness as seen from Zeacliff, near Zealand Falls Hut. It's hard to imagine that this area was once devastated by logging and fires. Jerry Shereda.

It is a more erodible rock than the harder gneiss and schist of the Littleton formation to the east. Various silicates (feldspar) are present in the decay of the monolith. As a result, the cliffs of Whitewall Mtn., visible across the notch from the hut, have produced large talus accumulations.

Conway granite was intruded into the overlying metamorphic rocks during the Jurassic period. The metamorphic rocks slowly eroded away, leaving the granite as the dominant bedrock species. Today, however, the igneous rocks are eroding faster than the more resistant metamorphic rocks still present in the Presidentials, so these western mountains are somewhat lower.

The mountains were scraped clean by the ice age glaciers. It is probable that the entire region was covered to

Skiing to Zealand Falls Hut.
Lou Lainey.

a considerable depth by ice. Exposed bedrock on Mt. Hale, for example, shows clear evidence of glacial scouring. Soils are thin, and bedrock is frequently exposed.

Ecology

Although Zealand Hut, at an elevation of 2,700 feet, is the lowest of the high huts, it lies in the spruce-fir zone. Many of the wildflowers along the rocky streambed of Whitewall Brook are common at higher elevations in the alpine zone. Bright yellow mountain avens (*Geum peckii*), usually found only at higher altitudes, are abundant. They are found only in the White Mountains and on one island in western Nova Scotia.

If you look carefully among the rocks along the streambed near the hut, you may also discover the tiny but carnivorous sundew (*Drosera rotundifolia*). It grows in moist but nutrient-deficient locations and obtains its nitrogen from unwary insects that become stuck on its sticky glandular hairs. It is an inhabitant of bogs; its appearance at Whitewall Brook is rather unusual. Sheep laurel (*Kalmia angustifolia*) is also common along the banks of the stream.

Painted trillium (*Trillium undulatum*), false Solomon's seal (*Smilacina trifolia*), clintonia (*Clintonia borealis*), and wood sorrel (*Oxalis montana*) are other species common in the nearby forest. Hobblebush (*Viburnum alnifolium*) spreads its flat ladders of oppositely arranged leaves along the trails.

The area immediately in front of the hut, just beyond the parapet, was cleared to provide a helipad when the hut was reconstructed in 1990. Here you can see the early stages of ecological succession when a cleared area is abandoned. Also note the nooks and crannies of the east-facing rock wall. In the morning you are likely to find a garter snake or two catching the warm morning sun.

For an after-dinner stroll, follow the self-guided nature walk at the end of this chapter.

Evidence of beaver activity is ubiquitous in the ponds and swales north of Zealand Pond along Zealand Trail. Zealand Pond itself is the largest of these. At times in the past, beavers could be seen at work, especially at dusk. But the beavers are now all gone from the valley, having been removed for fear of contamination of Bethlehem's water supply. (Beavers are notorious carriers of *Giardia lamblia,* an intestinal parasite.) Canada lynx are supposed to inhabit the valley, but I have never seen one nor talked to anyone who has.

Access to the Hut

The normal route to Zealand Hut is via the Zealand Trail, which is accessible from Route 302 near Twin Mtn. Access from the east is by the Avalon and Avalon-Zealand (A-Z) trails and by the Appalachian Trail from the south end of Crawford Notch.

Via Zealand Trail. The Zealand Trail starts at the southern terminus of the Forest Service Zealand Road, which branches south from Route 302 about 2.3 miles east of the traffic light in Twin Mtn. The road passes through Zealand Campground, past Sugarloaf Campground (both Forest Service campgrounds) and the parking lot at the road end 3.5 miles from the highway. The trail crosses Hoxie Brook and heads due south along the bed of the abandoned Zealand River Railroad. It stays to the right (west) of Zealand River, which is visible for much of the way. After following the roadbed for about 1 mile, the trail occasionally deviates, climbing through the woods and eventually reaching a series of meadows and beaver swamps. At 2.3 miles from the parking lot, the A-Z Trail

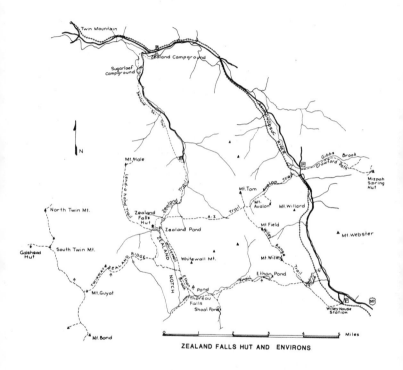

ZEALAND FALLS HUT AND ENVIRONS

enters from the left (sign). In a few hundred yards, Zealand
Pond is reached and skirted along the eastern shore. The
hut is just above the south end of the pond, but is not visible from the trail, though Zealand Falls can readily be
located. Just beyond the southern end, a trail junction is

reached (sign), and the Twinway to the hut diverges right, across the south outlet. In a few yards, the Twinway turns left and ascends sharply to the hut, about 0.2 mile from the trail junction.

The hut is 2.8 miles from the trailhead; the climb is 700 feet (the final pitch to the hut is 180 feet). Walking time is about 1.5 hours.

Via Avalon and A-Z Trails. Together with the Crawford Path, these two paths form the shortest route between Zealand Falls Hut and Mizpah Spring Hut. The route passes between Mt. Tom (4,047 feet) and Mt. Field (4,326 feet), providing easy access to both.

The trail starts at the Crawford Depot, a fine example of the importance we attached to rail transportation in the past. It is now operated jointly by the AMC and the U.S. Forest Service as an information center. Snacks and maps as well as toilet facilities are available. Off-road parking is available in a parking lot a few yards north of the depot. Crawford Notch Hostel, operated by the AMC, is just beyond.

After crossing the tracks and entering the woods, the Avalon Trail quickly passes the junction of the Mount Willard Trail (left). There are several local trails in this area and care must be taken to follow the main trail. The ascent is very gradual for the first 0.3 mile. After crossing Crawford Brook to the north side, the trail ascends more steeply. After a second crossing to the south side, the path climbs the south bank, staying well above the creek bottom.

At an unsigned trail junction 1.3 miles from the trailhead, the Avalon Trail turns south (left) directly up the north slope of Mt. Avalon, while the A-Z Trail continues southwestward up the valley. In 0.6 mile, the upper end of Crawford Brook is recrossed to the west side. The A-Z

Trail now leaves the brook and heads directly west to the Field-Tom col. The first branch trail to the right ascends to the wooded summit of Mt. Tom. In a few yards, the Willey Range Trail leaves left for the summit of Mt. Field.

The A-Z Trail now descends rapidly to the headwaters of Mt. Field Brook where it remains nearly level for about a mile, crossing several minor brooks and boggy places. It also crosses several snowmobile trails. After slabbing down on a moderate grade and crossing several small brooks, the trail swings southward around the beaver ponds north of Zealand Notch. After crossing the Zealand River, it meets the Zealand Trail, which is followed south (left) to the pond and the Twinway (right) to the hut.

The trail distance is 5.5 miles, and the total elevation gain is 2,000 feet. Walking time is 5 hours.

Day Hikes from Zealand Falls Hut

Interesting day trips from the hut range from a short, pleasant walk to Thoreau Falls to a demanding full-day traverse of the Willey Range. The hike to the top of Mt. Hale, another 4,000-footer, is rewarding, not only for the views from the summit, but also for the interesting geological history visible in the summit rocks.

Thoreau Falls. Late spring or early summer is the time to visit Thoreau Falls. This beautiful series of cascades and falls on the North Fork of the East Branch of the Pemigewasset River is at its prime when the river is full but is worth a visit any time of the year. It is the habitat for a showy stand of the bright yellow, waxy-leaved mountain avens and may be the lowest elevation at which this alpine plant can be found. It is an easy hour's walk to the top of the falls, which is almost the same elevation as Zealand Pond.

From the hut, drop down to the junction with the Ethan Pond Trail, which is followed right (south) along the abandoned bed of the Zealand Valley Railroad, a remnant of logging days. Wildflowers abound along the roadbed. From many points along the path, there are fine views of Whitewall, Zealand Notch, and the vast Pemigewasset Wilderness.

Near the south end of the valley, the trail contours across talus slopes full of debris from the Whitewall cliffs. There are also numbers of erratic boulders that were carried here by glaciers rather than riven from the cliffs by postglacial weathering. Down the slope toward the valley bottom, you can see glacial debris that appears to be a terminal moraine from a small valley glacier.

Shortly after leaving the talus, the trail reaches a flat where the Thoreau Falls Trail branches right. Dropping down slightly, the trail soon reaches open ledges at the head of Thoreau Falls.

Round-trip distance is 5 miles, with essentially no elevation change except for the pitch between the hut and Zealand Pond. Walking time is about 1.25 hours each way.

Summit of Mt. Hale. The name of the trail to Mt. Hale (4,054 feet), Lend-a-Hand, evokes images of tough scrambles up steep rock pitches and precarious traverses along narrow knife-edge ridges. The grade is actually fairly easy, but the footing is rather rough much of the way, particularly for those with heavy packs since there are many log bridges across a very wet section. The trail takes its name from a journal for charitable organizations that was edited by Edward Everett Hale, the Boston pastor and author for whom Mt. Hale was named. At one time the summit sported a fire tower, but all traces are gone now except for the concrete footings. Views are excellent from the barren summit.

From Zealand Falls Hut, go right on the Twinway to the north bank of Whitewall Brook a few yards to a trail junction. The Lend-a-Hand Trail starts here, leading straight ahead where the Twinway branches left and crosses the brook. After crossing a tributary brook, the trail swings northward and slabs gently upward across a poorly drained area, then climbs more steeply to the south ridge of Mt. Hale. More or less in the open, the trail follows the crest of the ridge to the bare summit.

The summit rocks are of igneous origin, representing an outcrop of the Moat Volcanic series. The rocks were extruded in the Jurassic period, and are related to Conway granite in the White Mountains. As the magma cooled, it developed a somewhat wavy and bubbly structure, which can be seen in the summit rocks. The basalt contains considerable magnetite, a magnetic mineral. Don't rely on your compass; the magnetite skews readings!

The summit also shows evidence of having been covered by ice during the Pleistocene. The gently rounded dome of the summit and the presence of glacial scour and polish indicate that the summit was deep beneath the ice.

On the return journey to the hut, avoid the Hale Brook Trail, which leads eastward to Zealand Road. Round-trip distance to the summit is 5 miles. Elevation gain is 1,400 feet. Walking time is 2 hours up, 1.5 hours returning.

Zeacliff. The most spectacular views in the near vicinity of the hut are from the open ledges at the east end of Zealand Ridge. From here the whole sweep of the Pemigewasset Wilderness is spread out before you. Evidence of logging a hundred years ago is still visible. If you look carefully, you can see gently sloping diagonal stripes on the wooded ridges to the south. These mark the location of logging roads or skid trails now occupied by lighter-colored hardwoods that contrast visually with the darker trees between.

In viewing this vast expanse of green, it is difficult to imagine how it looked 70 years ago, after rapacious logging and devastating fires. It is a tribute to the vast recuperative powers of nature that, to the untutored eye, the Pemi appears to be a pristine wilderness. Sitting on the rocks of Zeacliff, your mind can wander, recreating the scene of 100 years ago. Then logging engines hauled their cargo of spruce logs, and the woods echoed with the rasp of crosscut saws and the clank of hammer against steel as the logging rails pushed farther and farther into every corner of the drainage. Abandonment and fire followed, and the devastation appeared complete. But with sunlight, water, and seed, the process of regrowth is inexorable.

To reach the viewpoint, the Twinway is followed up from the hut. After crossing Whitewall Brook, the trail climbs steeply through alternating stands of white birch and dark conifer to the ridge crest, which it follows south. A loop trail diverges left to the cliffs overlooking Zealand Notch and the Pemigewasset Wilderness.

The round trip to the cliffs is about 3 miles, and the climb is 1,000 feet. Walking time is 1 hour up, slightly less for the return trip.

For an alternate return journey, the Zeacliff Trail may be followed to Zealand Valley. From the lookout, follow the west branch of the loop trail to the Twinway, which leads in a few yards to the junction of the Zeacliff Trail (left). This trail quickly drops off the summit ridge and descends very steeply (some scrambling down rocks is necessary). The route is not often used and is difficult to follow in places. Avoid paths that lead southward down a minor ridge. The trail heads eastward down the steep scarp of the west wall of the notch, finally crossing Whitewall Brook and joining the Ethan Pond Trail just below the talus slopes of Whitewall Mtn. The Ethan Pond Trail is followed north (left) to the junction with the Twinway and the short climb back to the hut. This route will add an hour to the total round-trip time.

Traverse of the Willey Range. For a good day's walk that includes two 4,000-foot peaks, try the Willey Range Trail. Follow the A-Z Trail east from the Zealand Trail at the south end of Zealand Pond to the height-of-land between Mt. Tom and Mt. Field. Here the Willey Range Trail diverges right (south) and climbs the northwest ridge of Mt. Field (4,326 feet) to the summit. There are good views of the Pemigewasset from the outlook. Mt. Field is named for Darby Field, who in 1642 became the first known white man to climb Mt. Washington (then known by its Native American name, Agiocochook).

The trail continues southeastward into the col between the two peaks, then climbs the ridge to the summit of Mt. Willey (4,302 feet). There are several viewpoints near the summit. Continuing southward, the trail drops very steeply to Kedron Brook. In a few yards, it meets the Ethan Pond Trail which is followed right (west) to the low pass above Ethan Pond. Eventually the Ethan Pond Trail swings north through Zealand Notch on an abandoned railroad grade and returns to the junction of the Twinway at the south end of Zealand Pond.

The round trip is a rugged 12 miles, climbs a total of 2,600 feet, and will take a good 8 hours.

Access to Adjacent Huts

Zealand Falls Hut lies between Galehead Hut to the west and Mizpah Hut to the east. The trails to both are fairly strenuous. The Twinway to Galehead is on an exposed ridge for much of the distance. It is advisable to be off the ridge early if thunderstorms threaten.

Twinway to Galehead Hut. The Twinway (part of the Appalachian Trail) departs from the south side of Zealand Hut, and follows the north bank of the brook for 200 yards before crossing to the south side and starting the steep climb to the ridge. Shortly after attaining the open ridge, a loop trail diverges left to spectacular viewpoints on the cliff tops, rejoining the Twinway via a continuation of the loop. The trail wanders over the flat top of Zealand Ridge and climbs gently to the south side of the ridge. A cairn marks a side path to the wooded summit of Zealand Mtn.(4,260 feet). Although the ridge is wooded, there are a number of viewpoints with fine views to the south. The trail swings south, drops to a low saddle and then climbs the north ridge of Mt. Guyot (4,580 feet). Although there is a bypass trail that skirts the summit to the north, the summit should be climbed if visibility is good, for there are excellent views from the bare ledges. It is a fine example of a glacially rounded dome, with Mt. Lafayette granite porphyry as the bedrock.

Two hundred yards west of the summit, the Bondcliff Trail leads southward over an open ridge to Mt. Bond (4,698 feet). The Twinway turns northward, descends about 100 feet, then continues northwestward on a mostly level grade. Much of this section is just about at timberline, with fine examples of krummholz, the scrubby but often very old tangle of red spruce and balsam fir that grows at the transition from timberline to tundra. In exposed places, the wind can be strong.

After crossing the broad wooded saddle between Guyot and South Twin, the Twinway slabs up the west side of South Twin, missing the summit by about 50 yards. Spur trails lead right to the summit cairn. The trail now starts down steeply for what seems forever, even though Galehead Hut can be seen directly below. After flattening out, the trail bends left and reaches a junction where the Garfield Ridge Trail enters on the right and the Frost Trail continues 40 yards straight to the hut.

Trail distance between the huts is 7 miles, with a total climb of 2,400 feet. Walking time is 5.5 hours.

Mizpah Spring Hut. The shortest route from Zealand to Mizpah follows the A-Z and Avalon Trails to Crawford Notch, then the Crawford Path and Mizpah Cutoff to the hut.

From Zealand, follow the Zealand Trail past the north end of Zealand Pond to the junction with the A-Z Trail, which branches right (east). After crossing the north outlet of Zealand Pond and skirting several beaver ponds, the A-Z Trail climbs gradually through an area in which there has been considerable recent logging. Eventually the trail starts the moderate climb to the Field-Tom col, where the Willey Range Trail takes off to the south (right). The A-Z Trail drops steeply into the eastern bowl, crosses a brook and soon joins the Avalon Trail, which it follows to the Crawford Notch Depot and Crawford Notch Hostel.

The Crawford Path leaves the east side of Route 302 about 100 yards north of the railroad station and heads eastward on the south bank of Gibbs Brook. Upper and lower Gibbs Falls are reached by short side trails on the left. After leaving the brook, the trail climbs steeply for a short distance, then slabs the valley side. The Mizpah Cut-off branches right, 1.7 miles from the road. After continuing to climb moderately for about 0.5 mile, the trail levels off and crosses a rather boggy area before dropping a few feet to Mizpah Spring Hut.

Trail distance from Zealand to Mizpah is 9 miles; the total climb is 3,100 feet. Walking time is 6 hours.

Winter at Zealand

Winter routes. Zealand Hut makes a fine destination point for an overnight ski tour. The vicinity of the hut also offers a number of interesting day tours as well as several more-demanding winter climbs. The hut is open during the winter and is supervised by an AMC caretaker. Overnight lodging and cooking facilities are available for a nominal fee. Overnight guests *must* bring their own sleeping bags and food. Although the access trail is readily negotiable by a cross-country skier of modest abilities, the trip should not be taken lightly. It should be remembered that White Mountain winter weather can be severe and can change from bright sunshine to a winter storm in a matter of a few hours. Winter parties, whether day-trippers or overnighters, should be equipped with sturdy touring skis or snowshoes, plenty of warm, weatherproof clothing; and a supply of emergency food in addition to their regular rations. Flash-lights (preferably headlamps) are essential, not only to cope with unlighted (not to mention unheated) dormitories, but also in case the party is overtaken by darkness on the way in. Remember that daylight lasts only 8.5 hours at the winter solstice and 10 hours in mid-February!

Given the necessary cautionary notices, a trip into Zealand in winter is an extraordinarily exhilarating and satisfying experience. No artificial lights blot out the sparkling specks of starshine that cover the sky. No signs of civilization are evident on the horizon; the sensation of isolation is almost palpable. The deep-woods quiet is broken only by the muffled sounds of Whitewall Brook, coursing deep beneath its snow blanket. Inside the hut, the after-dinner camaraderie of the common room is a welcome prelude to a deep winter sleep.

Zealand Road is closed to auto traffic in the winter; the trek to the hut starts at the highway. However, the road is open to snowmobile traffic and forms part of a popular route. Winter visitors may park in the large parking lot on Route 302, just east of Zealand Road. Although in previous years snowmobilers and skiers had to share the road, there is now a cross-country ski trail that keeps the two groups apart. The ski trail starts from the highway, about 600 feet west of Zealand Road. It climbs gradually, passing behind the first Sugarloaf Campground and through the second. The trail joins the road at the bridge, 1 mile from the start, crosses the bridge and reenters the woods on the west (right) side just beyond the Sugarloaf snowmobile trail. It crosses the snowmobile trail twice, when diverges south away from it. The trail climbs steadily, eventually rejoining Zealand Road at the terminal parking lot.

From here, the route follows the summer hiking trail (entrance at sign). The railroad grade is followed for about a mile. Although the old railroad crossed Zealand Brook several times, the Zealand Trail stays on the west bank, alternately joining the old grade and climbing more steeply through the woods. Eventually, the open meadows and beaver ponds marking the north end of the notch are reached. The trail winds its way around them, passing the

A-Z Trail junction before finally reaching the east shore of Zealand Pond. Most skiers follow the summer route to the south end of the pond and take the short spur trail (right) to the hut. The last pitch is too steep for skiing; skis may be left at the bottom and the short steep climb to the hut negotiated on foot.

An alternate route starting from the junction of the A-Z Trail can be skied all the way to the hut. This trail diverges right at the trail junction and climbs through the woods on the west side of the pond. The distance is the same either way.

Distance from Route 302 to Zealand Bridge, 1 mile; to end of road, 4.5 miles; to A-Z Trail, 6.8 miles; to Ethan Pond Trail, 7 miles; to Zealand Falls Hut, 7.3 miles. Elapsed time over packed trail, about 3.5 hours.

Many of the summer trails are traversable in winter only with snowshoes. It is possible to ascend the Twinway to Zeacliff and the Lend-a-Hand Trail to Mt. Hale on snowshoes. Skiable routes are restricted to the railroad grades that interlace the Pemigewasset Wilderness.

A fine day ski-tour from Zealand Hut follows the Ethan Pond Trail to Thoreau Falls. This is level most of the way, except for the gullies along the side of Whitewall Mtn., which at one time were crossed by railroad bridges. From the trail junction at the south end of Zealand Pond, follow the railroad grade south through Zealand Notch. Just where the valley opens out, the Thoreau Falls Trail branches right and leads, in 0.3 mile, to the top of Thoreau Falls, an open, ledgy series of waterfalls and cascades.

The round-trip distance is 5 miles; skiing time is about 2 hours, depending on snow depth and trail condition.

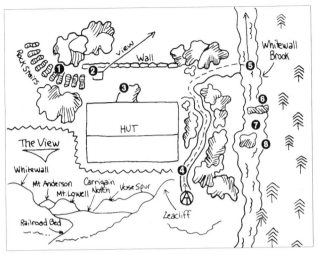

Self-Guided Nature Walk
Zealand Falls Hut
by Ray Welch

Station One

The walk begins about a third of the way down the rock stairs by the hut. Face back up toward the hut, and on your left is a medium-size deciduous tree. On your right is a smaller, shrubby tree. Their branches press into the path and the leaves of both nearly meet overhead. Do they remind you of maples? They are. Do they look like the same kind of maple? They don't and are not. The one on the left is red maple and the other is mountain maple. Mountain maple is a northern plant, common in cool woodlands, and is found even quite high on our peaks. Red maple is one of the East's most cosmopolitan and tolerant trees, found from Florida to Canada. The two species meet and mingle in the few places where the mix of climatic conditions allows both to live.

And here they are, living intermingled, both maples, both flowering each spring, but unable to interbreed. Evolution has made these relatives genetically isolated, even when they grow so seemingly intimately.

Station Two

Go back up the stairs. On the left at the top is a large squarish rock. Stand by it and look up the valley. Zealand Notch shows the classic U-shape that marks the eroding passage of the great continential glacier some 50,000 years ago. Carrigain Notch is also a U-shaped notch, its invisible part sketched on the vista panorama on the map. Younger shaping events were the avalanches that brought down some of the cliffs on Whitewall across the valley, whose rubble is still slowly being revegetated. At the base of these scars you can see a line of trees cutting across. This is the bed of an old railroad driven through the notch at the turn of the twentieth century by loggers. The rock wall you are standing on was put up when the hut was built, over a half-century ago. And here you are for a few hours. Why not sit down on the rock, rest for a few minutes, and enjoy the view?

Station Three

Extending out at the center base of the hut is a tongue of solid rock that slants down into the flat fill. This bedrock makes up all the rock you see around the hut, up the trail, out on the cascades, and across on Whitewall. It is Conway granite, an igneous rock which forms when melted rock deep underground slowly, over millions of years, cools. The slow cooling lets different minerals solidify as distinct crystals. Look closely at the rock. The chalky-white areas are feldspar, the glassy-gray ones are quartz, the scattered small dark flecks are mica. The block that marked Station Two is also a granite, but if you go back, you will see that it seems to have more mica—granites come in different blends, and there is more than one type. These are about 150 million years old, one of the youngest rocks in the White Mountains.

Station Four

Walk along the Appalachian Trail as it goes uphill on the south side of the hut. At the upper hut corner you can look out on a rocky meadow behind the hut, full of sun and weedy, nonwoody plants. The clearing is artificial, kept open by deliberate removal of invading woody plants. You are standing in a small grove of paper birches. Birches sprout successfully only in sunny spots. As they grow, however, their own shade prevents more birches from establishing, and shade-tolerant plants like balsam fir and red spruce then invade. This change in plant types, from weeds to forest, is called succession. In Zealand Notch the current major bout of succession began with the devastation of the old forest by lumbering and fire at the turn of the twentieth century. It is not over yet, and the birch stage is everywhere.

Station Five

Walk back down to the hut and turn right onto the cascades. Step across the water (if water level permits) and go down to the broad rock shelf overlooking the valley. Evidence of flux and change can be seen from far to near. If the air is clear, Mt. Tom, a couple of miles off, shows a grayish, curved line in the trees close to its top. This is a fir wave, a natural cycle of death and regeneration that sweeps through these mountains about every 75 years. In the valley below is a beaver pond, a short-lived pool that goes from pond to meadow to wood and back as beaver colonies come and go. At your feet, the rock is scoured clean by floods of meltwater or storm runoff each year. Here vegetation can barely establish itself before being swept to oblivion.

Station Six

Turn around. Upstream about 30 feet away is a rock face with a vertical side about four feet high. Go on up. On this flat, sunny surface are green patches of map lichen, much more commonly seen above treeline, but which also lives on rocks as low as this if light is abundant. Some colonies of this extremely slow-growing arctic and alpine organism, a combination of a fungus and an alga, have been dated out West as being at least 6,000 years old. How old are these? Not easy to say. But surely very old. Sprouting from rock crevices everywhere on the cascades are the large, glossy leaves of mountain avens. This plant is common on summits and sunny waterfalls in the White Mountains and is very rare elsewhere. The plant is thought to have evolved into this distinct species since the end of the ice age, about 12,000 years ago.

Station Seven

Continue to pick your way carefully upstream. About 35 feet above the previous stop and to the right of center of the cascades is a great block of granite about 15 feet wide and 8 feet tall. It is capped by a tiny thicket of plants. This block has managed to build up a thin film of soil on its top over the centuries, high enough to be safe from flooding. Here shrubs and even small balsams and spruces live, but they will never become great trees. Yet edge to the right and look up the cascade. A couple of hundred feet up on the left, a single large tree stands out on the skyline. This is a white pine (there is a much closer, smaller one to your right in the woods). Pines are very uncommon in this valley. This one grows in apparently not much more soil than on the rock block and is on a narrow "island" surrounded by stream and rock. Although its site seem precarious, this largest of trees around here just may have survived the fires and lumbering of a century ago because of this isolated location.

Station Eight

Go on a bit farther, or clamber—carefully—as far up as you want. There is much to see. The power of the water is obvious—smoothed rocks, sculptured chutes, dislodged boulders, and shattered ledges, with great worn cobbles filling bottoms of pools. But even in this dynamic and unstable habitat, evolution has produced organisms well adapted to life. The dark green, almost black mats that cling in patches to the rocks are water moss, an entirely aquatic plant. The rocks are home for much of the year to the larvae of the black fly. You may be pestered by the female adults seeking a blood meal. Once fed, the female mates and lays her eggs in the summer waters. The eggs hatch into larvae, which cling firmly to rocks in even the strongest currents, and filter their food from the tumult of the waters, waiting to emerge as adults the next spring. Even these apparent pests are part of the web of interconnecting species that time has woven in this valley.

9
Crawford Notch Hostel

▼

SINCE 1803 there have been hotels in Crawford Notch catering to the "destination" tourist. In that year, Captain Eleazar Rosebrook built a hostelry in Fabyan. Ethan Allen Crawford obtained this building, but it burned shortly thereafter, in 1818. Crawford quickly replaced the building and added to it over the years. Other hotels came, and in 1827 Crawford started construction of a large hotel at the head of the notch. It was completed in 1829, and Thomas J. Crawford, Ethan Allen's brother, took over as proprietor.

In 1852, Thomas J. began to build a new hotel on the present site of the Crawford House. But it, too, fell to the ravages of fire in April 1859. Not to be out of a summer's income, he rebuilt the structure, somewhat expanded, in 60 days. On the night of the Fourth of July, 100 guests were served in the dining room!

In Samuel C. Eastman's *White Mountain Guide Book,* published in 1869, the hotel is described thus:

> The Crawford House is a large and new edifice, very commodious and agreeable for a summer hotel. There are pleasant piazzas on the outside; and fine halls, much used in the evening for promenading, run the entire length of the house within. The parlor is large and well furnished, the dining-room ample in its proportions, and its table always supplied with the delicacies of the metropolitan markets, as well as such substantial articles of mountain production as delicious berries and the richest milk and

The Crawford Notch Hostel, originally the Shapleigh Studio, can be used as a way station between two high huts, Zealand and Mizpah. AMC Collection.

cream....Connected with the hotel are a bowling alley for rainy-day and evening amusement, and extensive stables, furnished with a large number of horses, to be used either under the saddle or in carriages, for the delightful rides about this vicinity....A more cheerful and pleasant resting-place cannot be found in the mountain tour, and visitors will find it agreeable to spend a few days in exploring the beauties of the neighborhood.

By 1875, the railroad from North Conway was completed through the notch to Fabyan; no longer was it necessary to reach the Crawford House by stagecoach. Fire, the scourge of remote mountain hotels, claimed it again, in 1977. All that is left is the Carriage House, which is used by the AMC as a pack house and storage building. In 1979 the AMC purchased the property to protect it from development, returning more than 400 acres, with the help of the Nature Conservancy, to the national forest and retaining the land that holds the remaining buildings.

The Crawford Notch Hostel, AMC's newest addition to the hut chain, is just south of the Crawford House site. It is located in the remodeled Shapleigh Studio and has two bunkrooms with accommodations for 20 and a central kitchen and common room. There are two adjoining bunkhouses that can hold 20 more guests. (Future changes may include renovating the bunkhouses and converting the studio into a visitor center and library.)

Strictly speaking, the Crawford Notch Hostel is not one of the huts; it is not a full-service facility. Hikers must bring and prepare their own food. However, it does have hot showers, a welcome amenity.

The hostel provides a good break in the long trek between Mizpah and Zealand. Although the distance is only eight miles, the hike is rather strenuous and the location of the hostel between the two is convenient. The only problem for the hut-hopper is that there is no food available; the nearest restaurant is at Fabyan, where there is a

Crawford Notch Hotel, in the heyday of the White Mountain grand hotels. AMC Collection.

motel. It is a good restaurant, but too far for walking and the hitchhiking is difficult.

Crawford Depot is a reminder of the good old days when tourists would detrain for the short carriage or taxi ride to the grand hotel. It has been restored by the AMC and the Forest Service and is now used as an information center for hikers and tourists. Maps, guidebooks, and snacks can be purchased here. It is also a major stop and transfer point for the AMC hiker shuttle. Reservations can made at the information desk in the depot.

Day Hikes from Crawford Notch Hostel

Most hikers use the hostel as a beginning or end point for a longer walk. However, there are a number of interesting day-hikes in the vicinity for the hiker who wishes to stay for a longer visit.

Ammonoosuc Lake. This pond is just a few yards from the hostel. A sign near the hotel site indicates the trail that leads northward. It uses an old road.

Saco Lake. The trail starts opposite the hostel and makes a loop around the east shore. It crosses the dam at the south end and ends at the highway. There are scenic views of the notch.

Distance 0.4 mile (not including the highway); 15 minutes.

Crawford Cliff and Gibbs Brook Scenic Area. The Crawford Path bisects the Gibbs Brook Scenic Area, a 900-acre nature preserve. The area reaches to the summit of Mt. Pierce (also known as Mt. Clinton) and the Presidential Range ridge. It was established primarily to preserve a stand of virgin spruce, one of the few extensive stands still remaining in the Northeast. The major species are red spruce and balsam fir, with some yellow and paper birch mixed in. On the ridge, there is a small strip of sub-alpine vegetation. There are no trails in the preserve except for the Crawford Path and Mizpah Cutoff.

From a parking lot about 200 yards north of Crawford Depot on the east side of the highway and just south of Gibbs Brook, the Crawford Path climbs steps and enters the woods. It stays on the south side of the brook, soon reaching a short side trail to a view of a small flume in Gibbs Brook. About 0.2 mile from the highway, the path reaches the junction of the Crawford Cliff Trail. This leads left (north), crosses Gibbs Brook and follows upstream to a small flume and pool. Leaving the brook, it climbs steeply to an old sign, where it turns left and ascends a rough way to a ledge with fine views of Crawford Notch and the Willey Range.

Returning to the main trail, proceed along the south bank of Gibbs Brook about 300 yards to a side path leading left to Gibbs Falls, a small but scenic cascade. Return by the same path.

Trail distance from the hostel is about 2 miles, including the detour to Crawford Cliff. Time, about 1.5 hours.

Mt. Willard. Mt. Willard sits at the very head of Crawford Notch, almost in line with it. The ledges near the top (2,850 feet) afford excellent views of the notch. Indeed, Moses F. Sweetser's *The White Mountains: A Handbook for Travelers* for 1890, says that the view "has a singular beauty and quaint individuality which no other view possesses. It is preferred by many frequenters of the hill country to any other prospect in the region."

In the heyday of the Crawford House, it was possible to ride a mountain wagon up a good carriage road from the

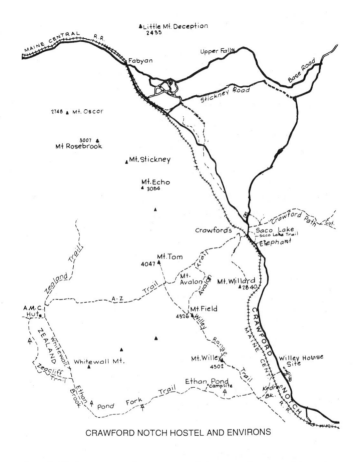

CRAWFORD NOTCH HOSTEL AND ENVIRONS

hotel. Today, no carriages carry visitors to the top, although the trail follows the old road in the upper part.

From Crawford Depot, the Mount Willard Trail coincides with the Avalon Trail for 0.1 mile, then turns left (south). It is level for a few yards, then the Mount Willard

Trail turns right and starts the ascent. In 100 yards, the trail bears right, bypassing a washed-out portion of the carriage road. In 0.5 mile, Centennial Pool is passed. It soon joins the old carriage road, which it follows 0.8 mile to the ledges east of the summit.

Trail distance from the depot to the summit, 1.6 mile; time about 1.25 hour.

Beecher Cascade and Mt. Avalon. Henry Ward Beecher, an abolitionist preacher and brother of Harriet Beecher Stowe, was an occasional visitor to Crawford Notch. In the mid-1800s he described in an article the pleasant pools and falls along Avalon Brook, which were later named in his honor. They are worth a visit, as is Mt. Avalon itself, with its fine views.

From the Crawford Depot, the Avalon Trail heads westward parallel to Avalon Brook. In 0.1 mile, the Mount Willard Trail departs left while the Avalon Trail continues straight ahead, ascending gradually. After crossing a brook, a loop trail diverges left to Beecher Cascade, after which it rejoins the main trail. At 1.3 miles from the depot, the A-Z trail diverges right to Zealand Hut. Now climbing steeply, the Avalon Trail reaches a col just below the summit of Mt. Avalon, from which a path leads left and climbs steeply to a viewpoint. Return by the same route.

Trail distance, to Beecher Cascade, 0.5 mile; to Mt. Avalon, 1.9 mile. Time, round trip, 3 hours.

Elephant Head. The ledges of Elephant Head form the east side of the gate of Crawford Notch. They consist of veins of white quartz in gray rock and are supposed to resemble an elephant's head. The ledges, which have excellent views of the notch, can be reached via the Webster-Jackson Trail.

The trail leaves the east side of the highway about 0.1 mile south of Crawford Depot. It passes through a clearing, then enters the woods and in 200 yards reaches the side path (right) to Elephant Head. The side path parallels the highway on easy grades to the summit of the knob, then descends a few yards to the ledge. The return is by the same route.

Trail distance totals approximately 1 mile round trip and takes about 30 minutes.

Access to Adjacent Huts

Route to Zealand Falls Hut. The Avalon Trail, which leaves from the Crawford Dept, leads to the A-Z Trail, then to the Zealand Trail and the hut. See pages 120–122 for a description of the route.

Trail distance is 5.5 miles; time, 3.5 hours.

Crawford Path to Mizpah Spring Hut. Together with the Mizpah Cutoff, the Crawford Path provides the most direct access to Mizpah. The trail leaves the highway opposite the Crawford House site and climbs steadily to the main ridge of the Presidential Range, then descends slightly to the hut. A description of the route can be found on page 151.

Trail distance is 2.5 miles; time is 2 hours.

10
Mizpah Spring Hut

From the Hut Log: August 29, 1965

> Spent last night at Lakes, and had planned to come over here by Crawford Path, but hutmaster there said no one was to leave the Lakes except by Ammonoosuc Ravine due to 25°, high winds, clouds, and snow. So went down Amm. Rav. to Base Station then over by road and up from Crawford House.
>
> **Howard Kellogg, Frances P. Kellogg,**
> **Jane Kellogg, Liz Kellogg, Tom Kellogg,**
> **David Kellogg, Bryn Mawr, PA**

WITH the completion of Galehead and Zealand Falls huts in 1932, the string of huts along the Appalachian Trail consisted of four in the western division and the four original huts in the Presidentials and Carter Notch. But there was a sizable gap between the two regions; it was nearly impossible to hike from Zealand to Lakes of the Clouds in one day. It required a good eight or nine hours, with a substantial portion of the walk above timberline. The decade of the 1950s also saw a steady increase in backcountry use, and the pattern was the same in the AMC huts: in the first year of the 1960s, hut use increased by one-third.

Clearly a new hut was needed somewhere between Zealand and Lakes, and given the increased foot traffic, it appeared that one would be financially viable. A suitable site would need to be about halfway between the two existing huts and near good water. A ledge above Mizpah

Built in 1964, Mizpah Spring Hut is the newest AMC high hut.
Judy Holmes.

Spring was considered; it was the most scenic location, but it was decided to reserve that site for "quiet contemplation, uncluttered by any building." Instead, the Forest Service and the AMC chose the site of the old Mizpah shelter.

According to Mudge's *The White Mountains,* the name Mizpah was originally thought to be a Native American word meaning "pillar in the wilderness." But the Bible is a more likely source; Mizpah in Hebrew means "watchtower," and there are several places in Palestine that bear this name.

The Mizpah Spring Hut was designed by Benjamin Stein, a Burlington architect with considerable hiking experience. The hut construction committee of the AMC and the Forest Service laid out the specifications; Stein designed the shell and the inner arrangement to accommodate the needs of crew and hut users. But there was more to it than designing an attractive building that would be aesthetically appropriate to the site. Because of the extremely high winds in the Presidentials, the hut was designed to withstand a 200-mile-an-hour wind! The roof also had to be able to support heavy snow loads.

The design included many innovations: a drying room for hikers' wet clothes, large south-facing windows to take advantage of the all-too-rare sunshine, bunkrooms of differing capacities to accommodate groups of various sizes, and an interior design to allow efficient crew operations and maximal user convenience.

The construction itself was a challenge. All of the material (including the steel roof beams) had to be transported to the site, except the foundation walls, which were built of the local gneiss rock. Strings of pack horses would have wrecked the trail, even if they had been available. Fortunately, high-capacity helicopters were available.

The dining room of Mizpah Spring Hut. Crew members often use songs and skits to entertain and educate visitors. Judy Holmes.

They could haul thousand-pound loads, leaving no mark on the trail. Over 17 tons of building materials could be airlifted in during one day. Construction was completed by the end of summer of 1964, and the hut was ready to receive guests by the opening of the 1965 summer season. Mizpah closed the gap between the western and eastern huts, enabling hikers to make the journey from Zealand to Lakes of the Clouds in two comfortable days.

Although Mizpah is usually visited en route to some other destination, there is certainly enough of interest in the vicinity to justify a special trip. There are several 4,000-footers to be climbed. It is close to timberline with interesting ecological gradients to be studied. The hut sits on a geological formation that is quite different from the areas to the west.

Geology

Crawford Notch lies approximately at the boundary between the granitic rocks to the west and the metamorphosed sedimentary rocks to the east. The four huts to the west (Lonesome Lake, Greenleaf, Galehead, and Zealand Falls) are underlain by granite formed from magma that was intruded 150 million years ago into the overlying Littleton formation. The eastern huts (Mizpah, Lakes, Madison, Pinkham, and Carter Notch) lie on the gneiss, quartzite, and schist of the exposed Littleton formation that was laid down 350 million years ago.

Erosion took its toll, but the schists of the Littleton formation were tougher than the granite and now form the highest ridges and peaks—those of the Presidential Range. Thus the youngest rocks are not the highest. But within the Littleton formation, the gneiss that underlies the Crawford

Path from the highway to Mizpah Spring predates the younger quartzite and mica schist found on the summit of Mt. Washington.

Although most of the lower elevations are covered with a thin layer of glacial till, bedrock is exposed in many places—along stream beds, above timberline, and in the immediate vicinity of Mizpah Spring Hut. The gneiss is a very hard banded rock, gray to rusty brown in color.

Ecology

The hut lies in the Canadian life zone. The dominant trees are red spruce and balsam fir, forming a dark and somber backdrop for the light brown building. Grasses and sedges cover the open spaces around the hut but have a hard time competing with the boots of trampers and frisbee players. Some of the flowers that are found nearby include the bright orange Devil's paintbrush, or hawkweed (*Hieracium aurantiacum*) and yellow mustard (*Brassica sp.*), neither native to this area. They were probably introduced during the construction of the hut.

A number of plants of the lily family grow near the hut and along the Crawford Path at lower elevations. Clintonia, or bluebead lily (*Clintonia borealis*), with its yellowish flowers and large blue berries, is common. Painted trillium (*Trillium undulatum*), with its three-part arrangement of leaves and flower parts, delights the early-season hiker. It is certainly one of the most delicate and beautiful of the early summer flowers to be found in the moist woods along the trail. In wet, boggy places, tall and succulent Indian poke (*Veratrum viride*) reaches nearly waist high. It can be recognized by the way its leaves clasp the stem. Another smaller lily, twisted-stalk (*Streptopus sp.*), also has leaves that clasp a jointed stalk. The flowers hang pendant from the lower side of the leaf on a slender stalk. Lily-of-the-valley-like Canada mayflower *(Maianthemum canadense)* is another visible member of the lily family.

Other flowers in the vicinity of the hut include diapensia *(Diapensia lapponica)*; pale laurel *(Kalmia polifolia)*, with its showy pink flowers; tiny, five-sepaled goldthread *(Coptis groenlandica)*; and the seven-parted star flower *(Trientalis borealis)*.

White-throated sparrows, ubiquitous near and above treeline, can often be seen and heard at the hut. Yellow-bellied fly catchers, gray-cheeked thrushes, and chickadees are common. An occasional Canada jay can be heard with his complaining squawk.

Snowshoe hares are rather tame and often can be seen feeding near the hut, usually at dusk or in early morning.

A self-guided nature trail has been marked in the vicinity (see the end of the chapter).

Access to the Hut

Normal access to Mizpah Spring Hut is via the Crawford Path and Mizpah Cutoff. This is the route that the hut crews use in packing supplies and is the shortest and quickest route from the highway. Approach is also possible via the Appalachian Trail and the Webster-Jackson Trail, but these routes are considerably more demanding. They both go over 4,052-foot Mt. Jackson.

Via Crawford Path and Mizpah Cutoff. The Crawford Path is probably the first purely recreational trail built in the United States. It was constructed in 1819 by Abel Crawford and his son Ethan Allen Crawford as a footpath. Shortly after it was opened, in 1820, a party that included

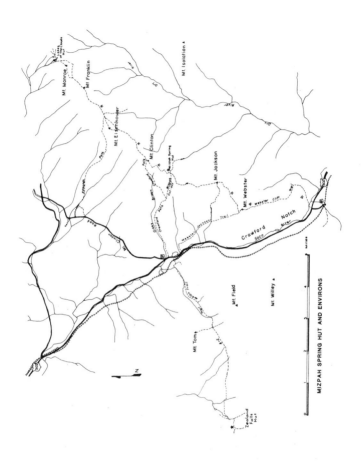

MIZPAH SPRING HUT AND ENVIRONS

Philip Carrigain, cartographer and former secretary of state
of New Hampshire, ascended Mt. Washington by the Crawford Path. Although the highest peak had received its name
in 1784, many of the peaks were yet unnamed. Carrigain's
party stayed on the summit for several hours, indulging in

an orgy of peak-naming: Adams, Jefferson, Madison, Monroe, Franklin, and (how did this happen?) Pleasant. Many years later, Pleasant was renamed Eisenhower.

The footpath was upgraded to a horse trail by another Crawford son, Thomas, in 1840. Today's path, no longer suitable for horses, follows the route of the bridle path at least as far as Mt. Monroe, near Lakes of the Clouds Hut. The lower part was extensively rebuilt in 1979 and has an excellent graded footway, although it runs through the woods and has no outlooks.

The trail starts from Route 302 just south of Gibbs Brook, about 200 yards north of Crawford Depot, opposite the Crawford House site. The former parking area just west of the trailhead has been closed, and the principal parking area is now on Mt. Clinton Road, near its junction with Route 302. From there the Crawford Connector, a spur path 0.2 mile long, leads to the Crawford Path. From Route 302, the Crawford Path climbs the highway bank on log steps and enters the woods. After about 300 yards, a trail leads left to Crawford Cliff. The Crawford Path stays on the south side of Gibbs Brook within hearing and occasional sight of the brook. It soon enters the national forest and Gibbs Brook Scenic Area. The path here passes through a fine stand of old-growth red spruce and balsam fir, thought by some to be the original forest. Mixed in are some extraordinarily large yellow birch trees and an occasional white birch. Shortly, a signed path leads left to Gibbs Falls, a scenic cascade with a fine, deep pool.

The path swings away from the brook and climbs more steeply, slabbing upward along the south slope of the valley. In 1.7 miles from the highway, the Mizpah Cutoff branches right and heads on a moderately steep grade toward the height-of-land just below the steep south slopes of Mt. Pierce (Mt. Clinton). The footway becomes nearly level, crossing boggy areas on log puncheons. About 0.7 mile from the junction, the Webster Cliff Trail enters from the right, the spring is passed, and the hut is just a few yards ahead.

Trail distance from the highway is 2.5 miles; the elevation gain is 1,900 feet. Walking time is 2 hours.

Via Mt. Jackson. For a more scenic route, with outlooks and views of the notch, the route over Mt. Jackson offers an attractive, if somewhat longer and more difficult, alternative. The summit of Mt. Jackson is open and affords fine views of the southern peaks of the Presidential Range. However, the trip takes twice as long as the shorter Crawford Path route.

The Webster-Jackson Trail leaves the east side of Route 302 0.1 mile south of Crawford Depot and 0.1 mile north of Gate of the Notch. In 200 yards, a trail leaves right to Elephant Head, a ledge overlooking the notch. The main trail heads toward the brook and ascends on the south bank. Shortly the trail branches right, away from an obvious path that continues up the south bank. A small brook is crossed, and, about 0.5 mile from the highway, a short trail leads right to Bugle Cliff, with fine views of the notch.

The Webster-Jackson Trail now climbs more steeply, crosses Flume Cascade Brook and in 0.5 mile reaches a trail junction. Take the left branch, which leads up the Silver Cascade Valley. The trail stays on the north side of the brook, crosses three small tributaries and soon reaches Tisdale Spring, just below the summit of Mt. Jackson. The spring is not reliable, but water may often be found a short distance below it. After ascending the rocky summit ledges for 300 yards, the Webster Cliff Trail is joined. The summit is open and affords excellent views.

Turning left (north) on the Webster Cliff Trail, the trail follows cairns before descending into the scrub. In about 0.3 mile from the summit, the trail enters a meadow from which there are good views to the east. At the north end of the meadow, the trail turns left and drops into the weeds and roller-coasters along the ridge. It finally meets the Mizpah Cutoff a few yards from the hut, which is reached by following the trail to the right.

The trail distance to the top of Mt. Jackson is 2.6 miles, and to the hut, 4.5 miles. Total elevation gain is 2,400 feet, and walking time is about 4 hours.

Via the Appalachian Trail (AT). This is a good day's walk, but there are good views of Crawford Notch from the AT and the trek is worthwhile if you have the time and energy and if the weather is good. See the AMC *White Mountain Guide* for trail descriptions.

Day Hikes from Mizpah Spring Hut

Mizpah Spring Hut is not often visited as a destination point; it is usually a way station on the climb to the summit of Mt. Washington. Nevertheless, there are several interesting climbs from the hut, including two 4,000-footers.

Mt. Pierce (Mt. Clinton). Mt. Pierce was originally named Mt. Clinton for an almost-president, DeWitt Clinton, who was defeated by James Madison in 1812. In 1913 the New Hampshire legislature apparently decided that this mountain should be named after a New Hampshire President rather than a defeated New York candidate. They renamed the peak Mt. Pierce "in honor of Franklin Pierce, fourteenth president of the United States and the only citizen or resident of New Hampshire who has been the incumbent of that exalted office." The original name remains popular and most maps show both names.

The summit of Mt. Pierce (4,310) is a flat dome of gray gneiss, rather open, with some views. While not a spectacular climb, in good weather the views are interesting and worth the trip.

The trail from Mizpah to the summit, which is part of the Webster Cliff Trail and a link in the Appalachian Trail, starts immediately west of the hut entrance. It climbs very steeply at first, past the yellow timberline weather-warning sign and up the steep south slope of the south summit of Pierce. After reaching an open area south of the south summit, it heads north, swings right, and enters the woods. After leaving the woods, it follows a line of cairns over the summit ledges. There is a large cairn at the main summit.

The return journey to the hut is easy, although there is considerable scrambling down the last quarter-mile. The round trip is 1.5 miles, with an elevation gain of 500 feet. Walking time is about 1 hour for the round trip.

Mt. Jackson. Moses F. Sweetser's *The White Mountains* tells us that it was William Oakes, Massachusetts botanist and explorer, who gave this mountain its name. He "sent his guide to its summit and had a bonfire kindled there to celebrate its christening." In the 1894 edition of his book, Sweetser suggests that Jackson be climbed by first taking the Crawford Path to Mt. Clinton, then "traversing the low ravine south of Mt. Clinton. The distance is one to one-and-a-half miles and the transit is very laborious, the way being frequently obstructed by thickets of dwarf spruce." Mt. Jackson (4,052 feet) is much easier to climb today, but it is also evident that a trailless ascent would be a rough scramble.

From the hut, the Mizpah Cutoff is followed a few yards past the spring, where the Webster Cliff Trail diverges left. The Webster Cliff Trail trends southward over the bumpy north ridge of Jackson, winds through a large meadow and finally climbs the scrub and ledges to the summit. The summit is open and affords good views of the southern peaks. The return by the same trail is routine and is described earlier in this chapter.

The round trip is 3.5 miles and the total climb is about 500 feet, despite the fact that the summit is only 250 feet higher than the hut. Walking time for the round trip is 2 hours.

Access to Adjacent Huts

Although it is possible to follow the Appalachian Trail to Zealand Falls Hut, the route is long and wearing, at least a 10-hour day. Even the shortest route, via the Crawford Path, Avalon, and A-Z trails, is a good day's walk. It is possible to break the journey with an overnight stay at the Crawford Notch Hostel (but note that the hostel does not have blankets or food service).

Route to Zealand Falls Hut. The usual route is along the Mizpah Cutoff to the Crawford Path, down to Crawford Notch where the Avalon Trail is taken to the A-Z Trail and then to the Zealand Trail and the hut. The route begins at the southwest corner of the clearing at Mizpah, across the stream to the trail junction. Keep right, more or less on the level across log walkways, then down to the junction with the Crawford Path. Go left along the graded path to Route 302 and the Crawford Notch Hostel and

Crawford Depot. From here, the Avalon Trail is followed to the A–Z Trail. At the junction with the Zealand Trail, turn left and follow along the east shore of Zealand Pond to the junction with the Twinway, which is followed, right, to the hut. A detailed description of the portion from the highway to the hut is found on page 120.

Trail distance is 8 miles with a total climb of 2,000 feet. Walking time is 6 hours.

Route to Lakes of the Clouds Hut. Except for the brief climb from the hut to the summit of Mt. Pierce, the entire route is above timberline on an exposed ridge. Although this makes for magnificent views, it also makes for hazardous conditions if the weather turns bad. Clouds often envelop the ridge, producing a cold, windy drizzle. It is not uncommon for windchill temperatures on the ridge to be 20° or 30° colder than at Mizpah. Nevertheless, on a sunny day with good visibility, the hike to Lakes of the Clouds is one of the finest in the White Mountains. The open ridge provides unexcelled views of Oakes Gulf and Montalban Ridge to the east and Mt. Washington and the main peaks of the Presidential Range to the north. Several minor summits on the ridge that the Crawford Path avoids should be ascended in good weather for their spectacular views.

The Crawford Path is also an excellent trail from which to view the alpine flowers. As it winds its way along the ridge, first one side and then the other, in and out of the scrub, the trail traverses the full range of alpine habitats. The early summer hiker is rewarded with magnificent displays of Lapland rosebay (*Rhododendron lapponicum*), alpine azalea (*Loiseleuria procumbens*), diapensia (*Diapensia lapponica*), and moss campion (*Silene acaulis*).

Please respect this fragile habitat by not creating parallel trails. Stay on the graded path while hiking. Waffle-bottomed boots are very hard on the vegetation.

The trail from the hut starts opposite the main entrance and follows the Webster Cliff Trail to the summit of Mt. Pierce (detailed description above). From the summit, the trail descends into scrub, where, in a few hundred yards, it meets the Crawford Path, which continues the descent into a low saddle between Mt. Pierce and Mt. Eisenhower. After slabbing to the left (west) of a minor hump on the ridge, the trail starts to climb the south ridge of Eisenhower. In a few yards, the Mt. Eisenhower Loop Trail over the summit diverges left, continuing up the ridge while the main path slabs the east side of the peak, staying in the scrubby vegetation. In bad weather, the path through the trees should be followed, but the views from the summit are worth the effort (an extra climb of 300 feet).

The two trails rejoin at the base of the northeast ridge and near this junction the Edmands Path from the Mt. Clinton Road also enters from the left. (This is the shortest route to civilization in case of emergency.) In a few more yards, the Mt. Eisenhower Trail from Oakes Gulf enters from the right. Water is found in a spring in the boggy area to the left (north) of the trail near this junction.

The Crawford Path now starts the ascent of Mt. Franklin. After a sharp ascent, the trail traverses a minor summit, then continues up the ridge, passing a short distance to the left of the highest part of the rather flat summit. The trail continues on a fairly level grade for some distance before starting the climb to Mt. Monroe. After gaining about 100 feet in elevation, the Mt. Monroe Loop diverges left to climb the summit. The main path continues around the south side of Monroe, traversing a narrow terrace between the sharp cone of Monroe to the left and steep drop-off to Oakes Gulf on the right. The trail then follows a relocated section, passing an area closed to public entry to protect the dwarf cinquefoil (*Potentilla robbinsiana*), an endangered species. The loop trail over Monroe rejoins in Monroe Flat and in a few yards the hut is reached.

Trail distance between the two huts is 5 miles. Total climb is about 1,600 feet if the main Crawford Path is followed, or about 2,200 feet if the summits of Eisenhower and Monroe are traversed. Walking time is about 3 hours, with an additional half-hour if the two summit loops are taken.

▼ ▼ ▼

Self-Guided Nature Walk
Mizpah Hut
by Ray Welch

To start your walk, go west on the Appalachian Trail (AT) toward Mt. Webster. Shortly after you enter the woods, you will descend a bit and come to a small bog bridge over a low wet spot, sometimes a small stream. This is Station One.

Station One

You are in dense shade. The trees that darken the ground are balsam firs and paper birches. The balsam firs are conifers and evergreens, while the paper birches are flowering plants and deciduous (although most people do not notice the flowers). The ground under these thickly growing trees is very dimly lighted and supports very little plant growth of any sort. The dense shade is responsible for this.

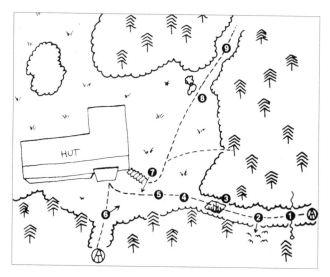

(Recall how much vegetation you see in the sunny opening around the hut.) The two trees here respond differently to the conditions their own growth has produced. There are young balsams here; there are no young birches. Birch cannot sprout successfully in shaded areas, balsam can. That birch is here tells you that the area was once much sunnier.

Station Two

Go back toward the hut about 15 feet. On your left is a slightly more open area with a dense carpet of green over the ground. This is a species of sphagnum moss, one of several species of this moss that are very common in the northern woods. It is a dampness lover and a bog lover. It holds water like a sponge, grows quickly and lushly, and is the plant responsible for turning ponds into bogs over time. The moss gradually grows in from the pond edges, replacing the water with mats of moss, mats so thick that the bottom layers die, compress, and turn into the dark-brown material we call peat moss when a bog is exploited for its semifossil moss. Although this spot is not a bog, a bog with sphagnum is nearby on the shoulder of Mt. Jackson, where the AT passes right through the Jackson Bog.

Station Three

Continue back toward the hut. Just before you come out of the woods, the trail passes over a flat rock slab about seven feet by three feet. Like all of the rocks nearby, it is a metamorphic rock, in this case, ancient ocean sediments transformed by heat and pressure into another form—here, gneiss or schist. All of the rock you walk over from here to the summit of Mt. Washington will be these types, not granite, as you might have thought. On the rock slab you are looking at now, you can see (if the light is right) faint parallel scratches or grooves that cut across it. These are glacial striations. During the last ice age, the great ice sheet flowed over this rock and sharp stones frozen in the bottom acted like rasps to scar the surface of the slab and show us the direction of the flow.

Station Four

Go into the opening for the hut. There is a bent-over iron rod in the trail and the rocky ground rises. Stop a few feet beyond the rod. Here you see the contrasts of sun and shade that woods and a clearing produce. On your right is a bushy clump of raspberry, and if you are here in late July (and lucky), you might find a ripe berry. Raspberry needs sunny spots to thrive. This requirement is part of what is called an ecological niche. All organisms, like the balsams and birches at Station One, have niche requirements.

Station Five

Go a bit closer toward the hut to the highest point on the rocky outcrop and then look down at your feet. Cutting through the rock is a dike of a coarser rock that is not eroded in the same way as the surrounding rock. When the main rock was being metamorphosed by heat and pressure far below the surface of the ancient Appalachians (hundreds of millions of years ago), these cracks formed and filled with melted material that, cooling slowly, had time to form the substantial crystals that make up the vein. The chalky, whitish material is feldspar; the more glassy, gray material is quartz (sand is mostly quartz); and the crystals with shiny flat surfaces, in layers like pages of a book, are mica. Under other conditions, these three minerals, melted, can cool to form granite.

Station Six

Stand by the sign where the AT enters the woods to go up Mt. Pierce (Mt. Clinton), but look back across the clearing, past the hut, to the summit of Mt. Jackson about a mile away. Weather permitting, you can see that the summit looks open, brushy, and rocky—not tree covered. Mt. Jackson is just tall enough (4,052 feet) to have a bit of tundra on its summit. You are standing, however, in a community called the boreal forest, typical on our mountains at midaltitudes (you are at 3,800 feet). Mountains compress climate, and the summits of the Presidentials have arctic conditions and the climate of Labrador, where conditions are so severe that trees cannot survive, only shrubby or nonwoody plants of the kinds you will see if you walk along the AT to Mt. Washington—an arctic island at the top of New England.

Station Seven

Go back to the hut and (with care) stand on the rock buttress built out from the corner. Look up Mt. Pierce, rising close by. Near the top you should see some obviously dead trees close to each other. If you climb Mt. Pierce, you will pass through this area of dead or dying balsam firs; if you hike to Mt. Jackson, you will see a similar spot halfway there. These are fir waves, cyclical patterns of growth, maturity, death, and regeneration seen throughout the White Mountains at these upper levels of the boreal forest. Terrible though it looks, it is not due to acid rain, hurricane damage, or air pollution, but is entirely natural. At a given spot it takes about 75 years for a cycle to complete. Look under the dead trees and you will see a new generation of healthy young balsam firs.

Station Eight

Walk diagonally across the "weedy" clearing—and indeed many plants are sun-needing roadside weeds, otherwise absent from the area—to where the trail goes down into the Dry River area. Just before you start into the woods, there are two rocks pushing up out of the soil on the left. The rocks are covered with green and gray, scabby growths. These are mosses and lichens, both considered to be pioneer species in the process of ecological succession. Neither of them has roots; moss is among the simplest of plants, and lichens are a symbiosis between a fungus and an alga. Not having roots, they do not need soil, and by colonizing rocks, they can actually aid in the formation of the humus and soil that set the stage for later phases of succession, stages seen everywhere around here if your eyes are alerted.

Station Nine

For example, continue on into the woods for a few feet along the trail. Once again you are among the same dim woods that you started in, and the rich meadowy community again gives way to close-packed, struggling young trees and a dark forest floor of tree litter and a bit of moss. Notice, however, a few stumps of larger evergreens here and there. Their rings indicate that they began to grow about 1940, probably following the windthrows of the 1938 hurricane that leveled so much of New England's woods. To keep the view open, larger trees are cut from time to time, but young ones attempt to replace their parents. As you return to the hut, reflect on the interplay between light and shade, disturbance and regeneration, the slow shifts of climate, and the even slower pace of geologic events, and you will become more aware that the time you spent here is but a moment in the measured process of change that is everywhere nature's most constant feature.

11
Lakes of the Clouds Hut

———————————————▼———————————————

From the Hut Log: July 26, 1973

> Phenomenal! Rugged people with craggy windswept weath-
> erworn faces. You can see a reflection of the beauty that
> these old people have seen in the twinkle of their eyes. The
> atmosphere that they create makes my soul sing for joy!
>
> **Cosmically Zapped**
> **Steve Van Gorder**
> **Westbrook, CT**

ON Saturday, June 30, 1900, William B. Curtis and
Allen Ormsbee started up the Crawford Path to ascend
Mt. Washington and join other members of the Appalachian Mountain Club who were holding a field meeting
at the Summit House. The weather had turned cold, but
they thought that only meant that it would be pleasantly
cool for climbing. Thickening clouds, however, signaled
the approach of a summer storm. By the time they reached
the summit of Mt. Pleasant (now called Mt. Eisenhower),
the weather was anything but pleasant. The two climbers
signed the register with the following entry: "Rain clouds
and wind sixty miles—Cold."

They were not worried, however. Both were active
and experienced athletes. Curtis had founded the New
York Athletic Club and was a well-known amateur athlete.
He had taken up mountaineering later in life but had pur-
sued the sport vigorously. He was a familiar figure in the
mountains—often climbing alone and clad in thin clothes

Looking down toward Lakes of the Clouds Hut and lakes, from the path leading to the summit of Mt. Washington.
Judy Holmes.

no matter what the weather. Ormsbee was also an amateur athlete and at 29 was in prime physical condition. So they continued their journey, ignoring warnings shouted to them by two local guides who were coming down the path.

When they reached Mt. Monroe, the storm broke. High winds and rain lashed the climbers. The temperature dropped, hovered near freezing, then dropped some more.

What was later called "the storm of the century" increased in fury. Sleet encrusted the rocks with thick coatings of slippery ice. On the summit, hurricane-force winds broke 40 panes of glass in the Summit House. Curtis and Ormsbee never made it. Both perished—Curtis near the Lakes of the Clouds and Ormsbee within a few hundred yards of the Signal Station at the summit. The storm lasted for 60 hours, finally clearing on Monday morning when search parties could venture forth.

The tragedy had an immediate effect. The AMC members assembled at the summit voted to construct a refuge near the Crawford Path. In the following year, Parker B. Field, the Club's councillor of improvements, scouted the upper reaches of the Crawford Path for a suitable site. In a letter to Benjamin Seaver, he wrote: "The refuge is to be of wood with ample accommodations for four persons, but with possible room for a dozen. It will be situated 100 rods beyond the point where Mr. Curtis' body was found and about 1/3 mile below the junction with the Boott's Spur Trail."

Money was raised and the refuge was built. A sign was placed over the door: "Not for pleasure camping." But it received heavy use by campers looking for a sheltered place to stay above timberline. In time, it became evident that a larger and more substantial structure was needed somewhere along the Crawford Path to serve both as an emergency refuge and as a place to stay for hikers making the long trek from Crawford Notch to the summit.

So in 1915 a stone refuge was built near the Lakes of the Clouds. It had a kitchen, bunk space for 36, and provision for a resident caretaker. The original building still stands today, but many additions and changes have been made since that time.

Today's Lakes of the Clouds Hut is the largest of the high huts, with sleeping accommodations for 90 in eight bunkrooms of various sizes. A small basement room accessible from the outside has bunk space for six backpackers. The large dining room, the newest addition (1968), is a light and airy room with large windows affording views of Mt. Monroe to the west and Mt. Washington to the east. A well-equipped kitchen permits the crew of eight to prepare the huge quantities of food needed to feed hordes of hungry hikers.

The hut sits in the low saddle between Monroe and Washington and has a commanding location overlooking Ammonoosuc Ravine. Although above timberline with extensive views in all directions, it is only a few yards above the scrub at the head of Ammonoosuc Ravine. So even in bad weather, it is possible to hike out to civilization with a minimum of exposure. Because of its location, it is visible from the summit of Mt. Washington and attracts numbers of day visitors. In good weather, the walk down from the summit is a rewarding one, with fine views of Ammonoosuc Ravine and the southern peaks of the Presidential Range.

Geology

An unusually good example of the Boott member (the layer of impure limestone between the upper and lower Littleton formations) lies exposed in the pass south of the hut and is traversed by the Crawford Path. As the result of folding and subsequent erosion, the Boott member in Monroe Flat is tilted vertically, with the upper part of the Littleton formation on the hut side, the lower part on the south side. In this area, the Boott member trends generally southeast-northwest. The summit of Mt. Monroe has a good exposure of the lower part of the Littleton formation.

Continental glaciation has also left its mark on the area. The Lakes of the Clouds were scoured out by the thick ice sheet that ground its way southeastward across the Presidentials. The lakes are shallow, not more than six feet deep, and freeze solid during the winter. Accordingly, there are no fish in the lakes.

During the continental glaciation, the entire Presidential Range was covered by ice as seen by the pockets of glacial till deposited on the summit of Mt. Washington when the ice sheet melted. When the ice sheet moved over the mountains, it broke off great blocks on the lee side, leaving the northwest slopes of Mt. Monroe relatively smooth and the steeper southeast slope a jumble of rocks that were plucked from the top.

Other evidence of glaciation can be seen in the glacial scour and striations on the rocks. The rock "nets" or polygons that can be seen in the flat area just south of the hut have been formed as the result of cycles of freezing and thawing that move the rocks outward from a soft earth center. Such nets can also be seen on Bigelow Lawn, just above the hut. With slightly steeper slopes, about 3 to 7 degrees, the nets become long block strips oriented downhill.

Ecology

Lakes of the Clouds Hut is an ideal base for exploring the ecology of the tundra. Within a few hundred yards of the hut are all of the major plant communities that exist in the alpine zone of the White Mountains.

Patches of krummholz—stunted, hundred-year-old mats of balsam fir and black spruce—grow just below the hut at the head of Ammonoosuc Ravine and in protected locations above the hut. A few yards farther down, the trees become erect and take on the character of a normal forest. Here the spruce is more likely to be red spruce. Mixed in with the conifers are occasional yellow and paper birches, mountain ash (not a true ash), and striped maple. But only below about 4,200 feet do the trees reach their typical height of 50 or 60 feet. Willow and birch may be found along the streams that drain the lakes.

Areas that are subject to strong winds and, consequently, little or no winter snow cover support dense mats of low shrubs. Typical members of this community include Bigelow sedge (*Carex bigelowii*), Lapland rosebay (*Rhododendron lapponicum*), diapensia (*Diapensia lapponica*), alpine azalea (*Loiseleuria procumbens*), and alpine bilberry (*Vaccinium uliginosum*). These are early-blooming plants and the hiker must visit the area in June for the spectacular displays of these flowers.

Where winter snow cover occurs, but is shallow enough to permit melting and disappearance in May, heath communities predominate. Bilberry, Labrador tea (*Ledum groenlandicum*), mountain cranberry (*Vaccinium vitis-idaea*), and black crowberry (*Empetrum nigrum*) are common. Where the snow does not melt until mid-June, in protected southeast-facing pockets, snowbank communities of alpine goldenrod (*Solidago cutleri*), dwarf bilberry (*Vaccinium cespitosum*), alpine bluet (*Houstonia caerulea*), and common hair grass (*Deschampsia sp.*) are found.

See the end of this chapter for a self-guided nature walk.

Access to the Hut

Although there are many ways the hiker can approach Lakes of the Clouds Hut from the highway, three are most popular: from Marshfield and the Crawford Notch area via the Ammonoosuc Ravine Trail; from Pinkham Notch via the Tuckerman Ravine Trail; and from the summit of Mt. Washington via the Crawford Path. Perched within sight of the summit, the hut is an attractive destination point for tourists driving or taking the cog railway to the top.

Via Ammonoosuc Ravine Trail. The shortest and most protected route from the valleys to the hut and the one involving the least elevation gain is the Ammonoosuc Ravine Trail. It starts from Marshfield, the base station of

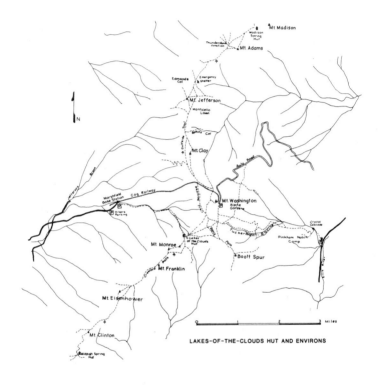

LAKES-OF-THE-CLOUDS HUT AND ENVIRONS

the cog railway, at an elevation of 2,500 feet and climbs directly up the ravine to the hut. Round trips are possible since the Jewell Trail leading to the Gulfside Trail north of Mt. Washington also starts at Marshfield.

The Base Station is reached from Base Road, off of Route 302 just west of Bretton Woods, or from the Crawford House site via Mt. Clinton Road. Hiker parking is available for a fee.

The trail begins at a parking lot on the Base Road, about 1 mile east of its junction with the Mt. Clinton Road and the Jefferson Notch Road. It follows a path through the woods, crossing Franklin Brook then passing over a double pipeline as it skirts around the Base Station area. It joins the old route of the trail at the edge of the Ammonoosuc River at 1 mile, after a slight descent, and bears right along the river, following the old route for the rest of the way. At 2.1 miles, the path crosses the Ammonoosuc River on a foot-bridge past Gem Pool, at the foot of a fine cascade. After crossing to the east bank, the trail starts to ascend steeply. Shortly, a side trail leads right to a spectacular viewpoint at the foot of the gorge. Above the viewpoint, the main stream tumbles down a steep and narrow ravine nearly 600 feet at an average angle of 45 degrees. Another similar branch to the north meets the main stream at the foot of the gorge.

Continuing the steep ascent, the trail passes within a few feet of the north branch of the river just above the junction with the main brook. The trail leads away from the brook, then toward it, crossing it and soon the main brook. This point is at the top of the main cascade. After two more brook crossings, the trail climbs ledges through the scrub and emerges into the open about 200 yards below the hut. Although the footway is well worn, there is a line of cairns here. The trail ends at the western corner of the building.

Trail distance is 3.1 miles with an elevation gain of 2,400 feet. Walking time is 3 hours.

Via Tuckerman Ravine Trail. The Tuckerman Ravine Trail is probably the most popular route to the summit of Mt. Washington and is a favored route of access to Lakes of the Clouds Hut. It climbs the spectacular headwall of the glacial cirque at the head of Tuckerman Ravine, one of the best examples of its kind in the White Mountains. The trail has some extremely steep portions that are slippery and require caution during wet weather. It is also exposed for a considerable distance from the base of the cirque over the plateau above and down to the hut.

The trail leaves from the southwest corner of the Trading Post at Pinkham Notch Visitor Center. Free parking is available in front on a stretch of the old road that is now bypassed by the highway. From the Trading Post (a pack scale is available where the trail begins), the path climbs by a gentle grade until it crosses the Cutler River on a bridge. Just beyond is a viewpoint for Crystal Cascade. The wide and heavily used trail continues upward more steeply now on several long switchbacks. Various trails to Boott Spur, Huntington Ravine, and Lion Head diverge, but the main path is never obscured. In about 2.5 miles, Hermit Lake shelter and the Forest Service and AMC buildings are reached.

The main trail keeps north of the stream and climbs the so-called Little Headwall. At the base of the cliffs south of the trail, the Boott member of the Littleton formation is exposed. After a sharp climb, the trail reaches the floor of the main cirque. At the foot of the main headwall, it bears right and ascends a steep slope, passing a snow arch that usually persists until late spring or early summer. This is an attractive hazard that has lured one person to his death and has injured others in narrow escapes. Walking on top of or beneath the arch is playing Russian roulette with tons of snow and ice. Chunks of the arch break off without warning. Stay away from it.

The trail climbs very steeply up the rocky slope on the right (north) side of the headwall. Many of the rocks are in unstable positions along this section of the trail and hikers must be careful not to dislodge rocks that may injure those below. And there usually are other hikers on this very popular route. If you do accidentally dislodge a rock, immediately shout a warning to those below. It may save a life.

The main part of the headwall has well-exposed quartzites and schists of the upper part of the Littleton formation. At an elevation of about 4,700 feet, near the top of the debris slope, rounded ledges showing glacial striations can be seen. These ledges were scoured by the continental ice sheet after the valley glacier that occupied Tuckerman Ravine had scoured out the cirque itself.

At the top of the talus slope, the trail turns sharp left and follows a narrow ledge for about 400 feet. This shelf is formed by one of the narrow black dikes that were intruded into the Littleton formation. After climbing over the lip of the headwall up a grassy slope, the trail emerges on top where the Alpine Garden Trail diverges right. In a few hundred yards, Tuckerman Junction, an important trail junction, is reached. Here the Tuckerman Crossover, leading straight ahead, is followed across Bigelow Lawn. (Do not turn right on the Tuckerman Trail unless you wish to climb to the summit of Mt. Washington.)

Bigelow Lawn has some excellent examples of alpine plant communities typical of windswept tundra. Low mats of diapensia, Lapland rosebay, and alpine azalea can be found. Three-forked sedge is abundant. Stone nets or polygons are common in this flat, exposed area.

From the western edge of the "lawn," the hut can readily be seen. The trail drops quickly, joining the Crawford Path and the Camel Trail just above the first lake. The hut is reached in about 100 yards.

Total trail distance from Pinkham Notch Visitor Center to Lakes of the Clouds Hut is 4.5 miles, and the elevation gain is 3,500 feet. Walking time is 4 hours.

From the summit of Mt. Washington. Lakes of the Clouds Hut is easily visible from the summit of Mt. Washington. It appears to be so close and so accessible that it is not surprising that many visitors to the summit elect to take the walk, expecting to be back up before the last train leaves for the Base Station. The crew at the hut welcomes day visitors and has soup and snacks available.

It is a pleasant and not difficult walk in good weather. But the trail is rocky and moderately steep in places. The footing is slippery in wet weather. And the entire route is above timberline on the most exposed western side of the summit. The weather can deteriorate rapidly, enveloping the summit in cold, drippy cloud. What begins as a pleasant walk in the cool sunshine can, and frequently does, change into an ordeal. Do not attempt the walk in street shoes or sandals; they simply are not adequate. You should have warm clothing and rain protection no matter what the weather looks like at the summit. If in doubt, check at the observatory museum or the service desk in the Sherman Adams building.

The Crawford Path provides the direct route from the summit to the hut. It can be picked up just north of the television tower where it heads north toward an abandoned stone corral. (Avoid a path branching left to a viewpoint near the TV station.) The Crawford Path heads first north-west, then swings west and descends to the junction with the Gulfside Trail. Following the left branch, the trail descends rapidly to the Westside Trail. The Crawford Path continues southwestward, heading directly toward the hut. Although there are numerous trail junctions along the route, they are well signed and there is no difficulty in keeping to the Crawford Path. Soon the trail passes between the two lakes and reaches the hut in a few yards.

Trail distance from the summit to the hut is 1.4 miles, and the elevation loss is a substantial 1,200 feet. Walking time down is about 1 hour, returning about 1.5 hours, con-sidering the 1,200-foot climb.

Day Hikes from Lakes of the Clouds Hut

Nearly everyone visiting Lakes of the Clouds Hut has probably just climbed or plans to climb Mt. Washington. The summit of Washington has something for everyone: television transmitters, a weather observatory, railroad, highway, restaurant, museum, parking lots, an old hotel (the Tip Top House, now restored as a museum), old foun-dations, and the new Sherman Adams building. It also has a view so spectacular that P. T. Barnum described it as "the second greatest show on Earth." Although surrounded by national forest, the summit itself is a state park.

Before it was Mt. Washington, however, Native Americans revered it as Agiocochook, "home of the Great Spirit." It got its present name in 1784, before General George Washington became president. Several books are available about the mountain's fascinating history: *The Story of Mount Washington* by F. Allen Burt (Dartmouth

Publications, Hanover, New Hampshire) and *Mount Washington: a Short Guide and History,* are just two.

The Mt. Washington Observatory, the only mountain-top weather station in the United States, has been operating for more than half a century. It occupies a portion of the new summit building. The observatory operates a museum on mountain weather and is well worth a visit. Membership is open to interested persons, and information can be obtained from the museum.

The cog railway was the first of its kind built any-where. Furthermore, it still has the steepest grade of any cog railroad in the world with the exception of the Pilatus railroad in Switzerland. Information about the railway is on display in the Sherman Adams building.

The climb to the summit of Mt. Washington and back via the Crawford Path is perhaps the least interesting trip that can be made from the hut. The route is mostly over the jumbled blocks of talus split off from bedrock by frost action. There is very little soil in this jumble and vegetation is sparse. Even bedrock is hard to find since it is covered by the talus to a considerable depth. Nevertheless, Mt. Washington is the highest peak in the Northeast and is therefore the inevitable destination of many tourists and hikers. Rather than taking the shortest way up and down, however, a more interesting circuit can be made by combining the climb to the summit with a visit to the Alpine Garden.

Circuit to Mt. Washington and Alpine Garden. The clockwise circuit is described, for the summit is reached first and there is a better chance of finding good weather in the morning. Take the Crawford Path to the summit by following the trail between the two lakes and slabbing the southwest slope of the summit. The footway is graded and well worn, marked with cairns and paint, and the junctions well signed; a detailed description is scarcely necessary.

To reach the Alpine Garden from the summit, follow the auto road to the left-hand curve just below the 7-mile marker. Here the Huntington Ravine Trail leads eastward on a gentle grade. The trail sign is a short distance in from the road (to discourage vandalism). Follow the Huntington Ravine Trail down to the junction with the Alpine Garden Trail at the north end of the Garden. The Alpine Garden Trail heads due south (right), dropping gently as it traverses the nearly flat bench. Although the Alpine Garden was once considered to be the remnant of an ancient peneplain (land worn almost level by erosion), more recent studies indicate that it may have been formed (and indeed is still being formed) by the slow movement of the rocky mass under the influence of frost action.

Whatever the cause of the Alpine Garden, it is certainly a botanist's paradise, especially early in the summer when the alpine flowers are in bloom. Diapensia with its five-petaled white blossoms, showy pink Lapland rosebay, alpine bilberry, and many more can be found. The flower buff should have both the *AMC Field Guide to Mountain Flowers of New England* and Bliss's *Alpine Zone of the Presidential Range,* referred to earlier.

Although the trail may cross running water, do not drink it. Drainage here is largely from the summit and is polluted.

After passing the junction with the Lion Head Trail at the southern end of the Alpine Garden, the trail contours along the head of Tuckerman Ravine and meets the Tuckerman Ravine Trail near the top of the headwall. Turn right and walk 200 yards to Tuckerman Junction where the

Tuckerman Crossover is followed, right, to the hut (see previous description above).

Summit of Mt. Monroe. This is a favorite after-dinner climb from Lakes of the Clouds Hut to help work off a big meal. The summit of Mt. Monroe exposes rocks of the lower part of the Littleton formation. Bedrock around the lakes is from the upper part of the Littleton formation. In between lies the Boott member trending in a southeast-northwest direction. Climbing Monroe from the hut, you cross the Boott member. On the summit, black-and-white banded gneiss from the lower part is exposed. You can also see the effects of the continental glaciation that moved from the northwest across Monroe, plucking chunks off the top and dropping the plucked boulders on the lee side.

The climb starts from the Crawford Path a few yards from the hut and ascends the northeast ridge about 0.3 mile to the summit. Elevation gain is 300 feet and walking (running?) time is about 20 minutes, more or less, depending on how big a dinner you ate.

Access to Adjacent Huts

Mizpah Spring Hut, Madison Spring Hut, and Pinkham Notch Visitor Center are all readily accessible from Lakes of the Clouds Hut.

Route to Mizpah Spring Hut. The Crawford Path between Lakes and Mizpah is certainly one of the most delightful walks in the Presidentials on a good day in early summer. The path is graded and gentle and traverses some of the finest displays of alpine vegetation to be seen anywhere in the mountains. Nevertheless, it is exposed for miles and can be grim in bad weather.

The Crawford Path is followed south from the hut along Monroe Flat, past the rock-delineated plant protection area, joining the Monroe Loop Trail at the southwest end of the summit ridge. The trail is followed over the shoulder of Mt. Franklin. It drops sharply into the nearly level col between Mt. Franklin and Mt. Eisenhower. At the south end of the col, the Mt. Eisenhower Trail from Oakes Gulf enters from the left.

In a few yards, the Mt. Eisenhower Loop diverges right and the relocated Edmands Path enters the Eisenhower Loop near this junction, rather than entering the Crawford Path directly as it used to do. This is the first exit route from the ridge leading to the highway and should be taken in an emergency. The Crawford Path slabs around the left (east) side of the summit. After dropping to the saddle between Eisenhower and Mt. Pierce (Mt. Clinton), the trail climbs moderately up the north ridge. Near the summit, the Crawford Path meets the Webster Cliff Trail, which you will take, left, to reach the almost indistinguishable summit in 150 yards. The Webster Cliff Trail continues on moderate grades down the southwest ridge of Mt. Pierce, eventually swinging to the left and dropping precipitously through the woods to the hut.

Trail distance from Lakes to Mizpah is 5 miles. Most of the way is downhill except for the 300-foot climb up Mt. Pierce, unless the peaks of Monroe and Eisenhower are ascended. The climb to Monroe is 300 feet and to Eisenhower, about 400 feet. Walking time is about 2.5 hours, with an additional half-hour if the summit loops are taken.

Route to Madison Spring Hut. The route is more or less level once the junction of the Crawford Path and the Westside Trail is reached. It is a spectacular walk in good weather, traversing the open ridge that arcs northward from Mt. Washington, then northeastward to its terminus at Mt. Madison. To the east along the entire route is the deep bowl of the Great Gulf, to the west the gentler slopes to Jefferson Notch and the ravines sloping north to the Moose River.

Because the route is above timberline the entire distance, it is exposed to the fury of summer storms. A number of trails drop quickly off the ridge for emergency egress in severe weather. The best advice is to check the weather forecast at the hut and plan to get on the trail early. There is not much water on the trail, so take an adequate supply.

The route follows the Crawford Path to the Westside Trail at an elevation of 5,600 feet. The Westside Trail contours the summit of Mt. Washington, passes under the cog railway trestle and immediately joins the Gulfside Trail. Go left at this junction. The Gulfside Trail swings northward away from the railway and in a few yards meets the junction with the Mt. Clay Loop (right) to the summit. The Boott member of the Littleton formation crosses the ridge at just about this point. (See cross section on pages 26–27.) If you climb the summit, you can see the rocks change from the mica schist of the upper Littleton to the banded gneisses of the lower portion. The band of change is, of course, the Boott member. The summit of Mt. Clay is a good place to see these black-and-white banded gneisses. Views of the Great Gulf are impressive from the several summits of Clay, but the trail is much rougher than the graded Gulfside. The traverse of the summit takes about 20 minutes longer.

From the Mt. Clay Loop junction, the Gulfside contours left to the Jewell Trail (a quick emergency descent to timber and the cog railway base station), then slabs downward to meet the Clay Loop Trail at the Clay-Jefferson col.

Several springs with good water are on side trails left (west) just before reaching the col. The spring area is boggy and usually has some interesting bog flowers.

The trail now ascends the south ridge of Mt. Jefferson, entering Monticello Lawn just after the Cornice Trail diverges left. Monticello Lawn is a miniature Alpine Garden that is interesting botanically and geologically. Stone polygons and other evidence of frost action are well developed, particularly on the south edge of the lawn. Although opinion is divided, Monticello Lawn probably has the same origin as Alpine Garden—frost action—and is not an ancient peneplain.

Here you can elect to climb the summit of Mt. Jefferson on the loop trail to the left or continue northeastward on the main path across the lawn. Climbing Jefferson adds about 15 minutes walking time. Either way, the trail crosses the Six Husbands Trail and drops to Edmands Col. This is an excellent place to see "roches moutonnees," so-called sheep rocks or sheep backs. These are ledges rounded by the scouring of the continental ice sheet as it ground across the col. The northwest side of each ledge is streamlined, while the southeast side is rough and steep, the result of "plucking" as the ice passed over the rocks. The bedrock here is composed of well-bedded schists and quartzites of the upper Littleton formation. At Edmands Col is a bronze tablet in memory of J. Rayner Edmands, who made most of the graded paths on the Northern Peaks. There is no emergency shelter in this col, and none of the trails leaving this area is a particularly safe escape route in bad weather. The Edmands Col Cutoff leads south, entering scrub almost immediately and is the quickest route to this rough form of shelter in dangerous weather. Another route would be the

Randolph Path north to the Castle Ravine Trail, which descends steeply over loose talus and may be hard to follow but is probably the fastest, safest route to civilization.

The Gulfside Trail now climbs the narrow ridge separating Jefferson Ravine from Castle Ravine and meets the Israel Ridge Path north of the low summit of Adams 5 (unmarked on some maps). The Israel Ridge Path is a quick way off the ridge to shelter at the Perch. The Gulfside continues northeastward over a grassy flat to unreliable Peabody Spring, then climbs gently to ominously named Thunderstorm Junction in the broad saddle between Mt. Adams and Mt. Sam Adams. This point is marked by a gigantic cairn that once was about 10 feet high. Several trails intersect here, including the loop trail to Mt. Adams, the second-highest peak in the White Mountains. The views from Adams are fine. The summit is also distinguished by the profusion of pointed and irregular boulders caused by frost action.

Continuing on the Gulfside Trail, now "paved" with flat stones and marked well with yellow paint, descend diagonally on a north-sloping bench between Mt. Adams and King Ravine. There are excellent views down this glacial ravine. Shortly after joining the Air Line for a few yards, the trail drops sharply to the Adams-Madison col and Madison Spring Hut.

Walking distance from Lakes to Madison is 6.8 miles. The total climb is about 1,300 feet, about half of that climbing Crawford Path to Westside Trail and most of the rest climbing the south ridge of Jefferson. Elapsed time is about 5 hours, exclusive of extra time required for traversing the summits.

Route to Pinkham Notch. Tuckerman Crossover is followed to Bigelow Lawn. Passing the junction at the

Davis Path, Tuckerman Junction is reached and the Tuckerman Ravine Trail followed, right, to the headwall. The descent is very steep and slippery in wet weather. The trail may be closed because of snow in early summer; check with the crew at the hut. After crossing the bottom of the cirque, the trail drops down the Little Headwall and into the flat area at Hermit Lake where there are several buildings and a number of shelters. Radio communication is available in an emergency. The trail, now a main route traversed by thousands of hikers in the summer and skiers in the winter, drops rapidly to the highway at the AMC Pinkham Notch Visitor Center.

Trail distance is 4 miles, and the elevation gain is about 500 feet (from the hut to Bigelow Lawn). Walking time is about 3 hours.

▼ ▼ ▼

Self-Guided Nature Walk
Lakes of the Clouds Hut
by Ray Welch

Go outside the hut and proceed to the southeast corner by the Ammonoosuc Ravine Trail sign. This is Station One.

Station One

From the corner of the hut, look up Mt. Monroe and notice that the slope to the left is much steeper than the one on the right. This is no accident. During the last ice age the great continental ice sheet overrode the Presidentials, sliding over Mt. Monroe from northwest to southeast. The relentless ice, its bottom melting slightly and then refreezing as it

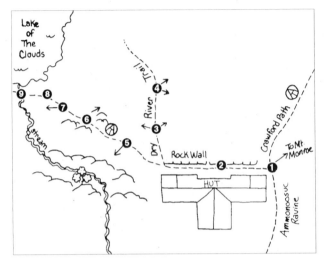

was forced up and over to the lee side of the mountain,
pried out weaker rocks, seized them firmly, and swept them
off, leaving the gnawed-away look seen now. Studies of the
sediments in the larger Lake of the Clouds show that the ice
receded from the peaks about 12,000 years ago. The climate at the end of the ice age was so severe that the freezing and thawing cycles of that time left the rubble of
boulders that litter the slopes everywhere today.

Station Two

Along the hut foundation you can spot some healthy dandelions. This alien weed is doing well, but only because of
the microclimate the hut provides. The stone wall faces
southwest and is a warm suntrap; the hut shields the spot
from the prevailing winds and is deeply snow-protected in
the winter. So the dandelions—seeds perhaps blown up

from the valley—survive, thrive, and reproduce. They can invade a few feet farther out on the tundra, but beyond that there are none, since the stress of the normal tundra climate lets only natives survive. The tundra plants you see, dominated by heaths (azalea relatives), rushes, and sedges, plus some others, were marooned here as the ice retreated.

Station Three

Walk up the Dry River Trail about 25 feet and look both near and far. The rocky, grassy appearance of the terrain is typical of most of our tundra. Yet the plain, grasslike plant everywhere is not a grass. It is Bigelow sedge, named for Jacob Bigelow, its discoverer. The differences between sedges and grasses are subtle, based largely on flower structure, and obvious only to botanists. Bigelow sedge is perhaps the most abundant plant on the tundra.

Station Four

Walk a few feet more up the trail and you will see some low-lying mounds of a dark green, waxy-leaved plant, reminiscent, perhaps, of Astroturf. This is diapensia, a shrublet of the high Arctic in both the Old and New worlds. This plant is found in Scandinavia as well as here, showing that the high Arctic is really one biological community, even across oceans. These low mounds are, indeed, shrubs. Lying so low, even fierce winds slide harmlessly over, and the evergreen, leathery leaves help conserve water. Diapensia blooms profusely in early June, then spends the rest of the short summer storing up energy for next year's attempt. You can see convergent evolution among our alpine plants here since an unrelated shrub, the alpine azalea, has almost exactly the same appearance as diapensia when not in bloom. Tough though these plants look, they resent being stepped on. Stay on the trail.

Station Five

Return to the Crawford Path and walk along it toward Mt. Washington. To your left, about 50 feet away is a tiny stream tumbling among the rocks. Here water-loving arctic plants thrive, like willows, sedges, and birches, as well as some lowland plants that find shelter there, like meadowsweet. You can also see, even from the trail, the lustrous, large, rounded leaves (and in midsummer, the yellow, buttercuplike flowers) of mountain avens. Abundant here, it is absent from the Arctic, probably having evolved in the Presidentials since the end of the ice age. It is common by sunny waterfalls below timberline, too. Much less common, indeed very rare and found only in the White Mountains, is dwarf cinquefoil, with a population of about a thousand individuals on Monroe Flats. In early June this minute plant produces yellow flowers, but they are much smaller than those of mountain avens. Both plants are in the rose family.

Station Six

A little farther on, take a look at the rocks near the trail. The rocks themselves are mostly schist, a metamorphosed sedimentary rock that makes up almost all of the rock from here to the summit. In their natural state, these rocks are gray, with sparkling crystals of mica, but most are heavily covered with crusty splotches in shades of gray, black, or green. These are colonies of different species of lichen, a plantlike organism in which certain fungi and algae have set up a mutual household, growing together in the colony you see. Acting like a single organism, lichens are very hardy, but very slow growing. The green, paintlike splotches are map lichen, so common on tundra rocks that they tint them at a distance, and each colony could well be some centuries old. Faster-growing lichens are scattered through the tundra among the vegetation. Very common is Iceland lichen, which is brown when dry and olive when damp, looking almost spongelike or like tiny, leafless shrubs. The branches of these can grow millimeters a year.

Station Seven

As you go on, look at the rock outcropping to the left a couple of hundred feet away. There you will see huddled in the lee of the weathered blocks the shrubby growths called krummholz ("twisted wood"), which are not shrubs at all, but dwarfed trees, mostly balsam fir. Their existence on the tundra in only this sheltered spot reflects the harshness of the climate, since the flying snow, drying wind, and freezing fog of exposed tundra will push them beyond the brink of survival. So they dwell meagerly behind these rocky refuges, shielded from the worst of the stresses, and have done so for centuries. Even so, when some have been cut down to count the tree rings, none is more than about 150 years old; but these surely represent the current sprouts from branches that have taken root as the old trunks die off. If the climate does not change, it is possible that these plants can exist as the same genetic individual indefinitely.

Station Eight

Continue a few feet farther and stop. The vista is one of sky and rock, water and air. The tundra lies around you and, except for the wind, is probably quite silent; you rarely hear an animal noise, and you are unlikely to see an animal. But there is animal life here. On sunny days you might see black spiders scuttle out of your way as you walk; in July the White Mountain butterfly, found only here, flutters in its mating rituals; the dark-gray and white Junco perches on rocks and branches; the white-throated sparrow, a brownish bird, sings its clear notes; ravens can soar overhead; even woodchucks live in the rocks above the lakes. But you are the largest animal on the tundra, a giant among dwarfs.

Station Nine

Walk to where the trail crosses the outlet of lower Lake of the Clouds and end your hike there with some shoreline thoughts. The lake has been here for but an eyeblink of time, gouged out by the last glaciers and first filled with its melting 12,000 years ago. The lake has no fish but is home to a few plants, some aquatic insects, and a colony of spring peepers, frogs whose mating calls can be heard even on midsummer evenings, for summer barely comes here. All the life of the lake and the tundra must hasten to do its work in the short time when water is briefly unlocked from ice and the sun again brings it reviving touch.

12
Madison Spring Hut

▼

From the Hut Log: June 15, 1960

> I am having a new 50 star flag flown over the Supreme
> Court Building, Wash. DC on July 4, 1960 and sending it
> to Madison Hut in appreciation of the wonderful hospitali-
> ty of the crew on my visit here.
>
> **William O. Douglas, Wash. DC**

EARLY in the evening of October 7, 1940, AMC Huts
Manager Joe Dodge received a telephone call at
Pinkham Notch Camp from the manager of the Ravine
House in Randolph. There was a bright glow in the sky
somewhere high on the northern ridge of the Presidentials.
It was dark and the location of the fire could not be pin-
pointed. But it was dishearteningly close to the Madison-
Adams col, where Madison Spring Hut was located.

Dodge went outside to scan the sky to the north but
too many ridges intervened; nothing could be seen. Then
from the Glen House, on the highway north of Pinkham
Notch Camp, came word that a faint glow could be seen,
but on the Randolph side of the ridge. This almost certainly meant that Madison Hut was burning. There was little
else in the vicinity that could burn so vigorously. A few
minutes later one of the hutmen arrived at the Ravine
House after running down the Valley Way. The news was
bad: a flash fire had started when the hutmen were trans-
ferring gasoline in the kitchen. Two fire extinguishers had
been emptied on the blaze to no avail. Madison Hut, the

Looking down on the Madison Spring Hut with Mt. Madison behind. Judy Holmes.

original AMC shelter, which had stood on the crest of the Presidentials for 52 years, was aflame.

The two hutmen and their three guests managed to escape with their personal effects, but nothing else. When the fire finally died down, nothing was left but the masonry walls and a pile of stove parts and kitchen utensils scattered on the ground. Madison Hut was no more!

But the masonry walls were standing and repairable. And "Number 2," the small adjacent hut that had been used for storage, was still intact. The job of rebuilding the hut began immediately. The debris was carried down, the site was cleaned, and plans were drawn for the new hut. Reconstruction began the following spring.

With the help of donkeys and shoulder pads borrowed from the local high school football team, Joe Dodge and his crew hauled 50 tons of materials up the mountain in a six-week period. Joe Dodge's fanatic zeal in keeping the hut system operating paid a substantial dividend; on August 2, 1941, Dodge held a housewarming at the new hut. Madison was ready to receive guests once again.

That structure still stands today—a monument to the extraordinary ability and dedication of Joe Dodge. It has recently been expanded and reconstructed. The hut sleeps 50 in two bunkrooms. The sleeping quarters occupy the upper end of a "T" with the kitchen and crew quarters at the bottom and the dining room in between. It is located just north of the col between Mt. Madison and Mt. Adams, just above timberline.

Geology

Madison Spring Hut sits on the surface of the upper Littleton formation. Here the bedrock is a micaceous schist that

Madison Spring Hut in 1906. Back then hikers were called "trampers", the word "backpacking" had not been coined.
AMC Collection.

was extensively folded in the Devonian period. Many of the nearby peaks have good exposures showing these folds. Excellent examples of white quartz rocks, formed when gaseous magma cooled and crystallized in cracks in the existing bedrock, can be found nearby. Evidence of continental glaciation is abundant in the vicinity of the hut. The peaks are rounded, and summit bedrock shows glacial striations that were formed as the ice sheet ground across the region. The striations here indicate that the ice moved from the northwest to the southeast.

Evidence of active valley glaciers can also be seen in the area, notably in King Ravine, northwest of the hut.

Ecology

The hut lies just above timberline, and the plants in the vicinity are typical of the Presidential Range tundra. The krummholz, here primarily balsam fir, extends up Snyder Brook to occupy protected areas around the hut. Arctic willow and dwarf birch can also be found. Diapensia, Lapland rosebay, and alpine azalea form mats of vegetation in protected areas between the rocks. Indian poke can sometimes be spotted growing under the protective cover of balsam fir.

Lichens cover most of the rocks. The greenish map lichen is so widespread that it gives a greenish cast to the immediate landscape. A black fruticose lichen adorns some of the rocks. In addition to its color, it can be recognized by its habit of growing on single short stalks. It can be readily peeled from the rocks whereas the green map lichen is tightly appressed to the rock surface. There is one lichen here that occupies an unusual ecological niche: a brown lichen that grows on the walls of the hut. Why only on the walls? Because it needs the calcium that is leached from the mortar holding the stone walls in place.

Access to the Hut

The easiest access to the hut from the highway is from the north via the Valley Way. It follows the ravine down which Snyder Brook flows northward from the Madison-Adams col. The path crosses the Snyder Brook Scenic Area, a 36-acre preserve originally purchased by the AMC and later donated to the White Mountain National Forest.

Via the Valley Way. The trail starts from the parking lot at Appalachia on the south side of U.S. Route 2. After crossing the railroad tracks, the Valley Way leads left across the power-line right of way, while the Air Line branches right. In a few yards, Maple Walk diverges left from the main path to join the Fallsway. The waterfall exposes a fine specimen of black-banded volcanic rock of the Ammonoosuc series. These are very old rocks that were deposited in the Ordovician period, 400 million years ago. Farther up, the Fallsway joins the Valley Way, then in a few yards branches left for a worthwhile loop to Tama Fall. The waterfall and cascades are located in a fine exposure of Bickford granite. This fine-grained granite was intruded in late Devonian time, 300 million years ago, after the great folding of that period.

Just above Tama Fall, the Fallsway rejoins the Valley Way. (There is a great profusion of trails in this area, but they are well marked and signed at all junctions.)

Staying close to the brook, the Valley Way is soon joined by Beechwood Way from the right. In another 30 yards, the Brookside continues straight while the Valley Way turns right. In 100 yards, the Randolph Path crosses.

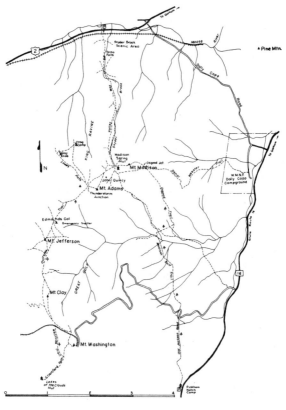

MADISON SPRING HUT AND ENVIRONS

(This trail leads from the Randolph East parking area on the Dolly Copp Road to Edmands Col.) The Valley Way now climbs a ridge west of the brook. In about 1.2 miles, the Scar Trail diverges right, and in another 0.3 mile the Watson Path crosses.

The Valley Way now climbs above the stream, slabbing the steep eastern side of Durand Ridge. A side trail (Lower Bruin) branches left to Bruin Rock and Duck Fall. In 0.3 mile a path on the right formerly led to Valley Way Campsite, which is currently closed. In a few hundred yards, Valley Way passes a spring to the right of the trail. The next trail junction is with the Upper Bruin Trail, which leads right to join the Air Line at the lower end of the Knife Edge along the upper part of Durand Ridge. Staying close to Snyder Brook, the Valley Way steepens and enters the scrub just below the hut. As you come up over a rise, the hut can be seen directly ahead.

The Valley Way is well marked and well traveled. However, the hiker who wants to keep the various trails sorted out should obtain a copy of the Randolph Mountain Club map, *Randolph Valley and the Northern Peaks.* This is available at Pinkham Notch Visitor Center and Madison Spring Hut. The 1989 map, *Mount Washington and the Heart of the Presidential Range* shows, at a scale of 1:20,000, shows all of the various trails intersecting the Valley Way.

Trail distance from the parking lot to the hut is 3.8 miles, and the elevation gain is 3,500 feet. Time to Randolph Path is 45 minutes; to the Watson Path, 2 hours; to Upper Bruin, 3 hours; and to the hut, 3.5 hours.

Via Daniel Webster–Scout Trail. This trail provides access to the hut from Dolly Copp Campground, near the junction of Dolly Copp Road and Route 16. The Great Gulf Link and Trail, together with the Osgood Path, can also be used to reach the hut from the campground. The Daniel Webster–Scout Trail begins near the south end of the main campground road and strikes westward directly up the slope. It climbs on a moderate grade for about 2 miles. At about the

3,000-foot contour, the grade steepens and the forest changes abruptly from hardwoods to evergreens. In about 0.5 mile, the last sure water is encountered, although water is usually found farther along the trail. At 2.9 miles it begins a very steep and rough climb nearly straight up the slope.

Soon after entering the scrub, Osgood Junction is reached. Here the Daniel Webster–Scout Trail continues, right, to the summit of Mt. Madison (5,367 feet), while the Osgood Trail comes in from the left. The direct route to the hut is along the Parapet Trail, marked with blue paint blazes, which leads west from the junction. It contours the south side of the Madison cone and joins the Madison Gulf Trail where the latter leaves the scrub at the head of Madison Gulf. The Madison Gulf Trail is then followed, right, over the Parapet, to the Star Lake Trail, and to the hut.

Trail distance is 4.5 miles, and the elevation gain is 3,500 feet. Time to Osgood Junction is about 3.5 hours; to the hut via the Parapet Trail, 4 hours. The alternate route over the summit requires an additional 20 minutes.

Day Hikes from Madison Spring Hut

Mt. Madison via the Osgood Trail. Mt. Madison is the northernmost peak of the Presidential Range. It is readily accessible from Madison Spring Hut with a modest climb of 500 feet. The Osgood Trail is followed east from the hut to the crest of the southwest ridge. There it swings a little north of east and ascends the ridge a little south of the crest. Madison Gulf is on the right. A few yards from the summit, the trail turns left and climbs the ridge, which it follows to the summit cairn.

The steep summit is composed largely of huge talus blocks. Near the top, bedrock is exposed, consisting of the upper part of the Littleton formation. Folds in the bedded schists and quartzites are quite evident. Osgood Ridge, extending southeast from the summit, consists of a series of folds in the schists, represented by the individual knobs along the ridge. Howker Ridge, stretching northeast from the summit, displays fine examples of bedding, jointing foliation, and folding in the Littleton formation rocks.

A good route back to the hut is down Osgood Ridge to Osgood Junction, then back to the Madison Gulf Trail via the Parapet and Star Lake trails. The hut is 0.1 mile north of the Madison Gulf Trail.

Distance from the hut to the summit is 0.5 mile, the elevation gain is 500 feet, and the climbing time is about 30 minutes. Round trip via the Osgood, Parapet, and Madison Gulf trails is 2 miles and takes about 1.5 hours.

Mt. Adams via Star Lake Trail. Mt. Adams (5,774 feet) is the highest peak in the Northern Presidentials and the second-highest peak in New England. It is the most striking of the northern peaks, and in many ways rivals its higher neighbor to the south in interest. The mountain has no fewer than four minor peaks in addition to the main summit: John Quincy Adams (5,410 feet), Sam Adams (5,585 feet), Adams 4 (5,355 feet), and Adams 5 (5,360 feet—unmarked on some maps). Four glacial cirques cut into its sides; massive ridges stretch northward into the Moose River Valley. The main summit is interesting not only for its spectacular views but also for the fine examples of folding in the Littleton formation dating back to the Devonian period and much more recent glacial activity.

The summit is most quickly reached via the Star Lake Trail, which leads south from the hut in common with the Parapet Trail for 200 yards, then branches right, passing west of Star Lake, a boggy glacial tarn. Climbing about 100 feet in elevation, the Star Lake Trail reaches the Adams-Madison col about 0.3 mile from the hut. The Buttress Trail diverges left here. The Star Lake Trail slabs up the steep southeastern slope of John Quincy Adams, finally swinging around to the northwest and climbing, with some fairly difficult scrambles, the last 200 feet to the summit.

For the return trip, the Air Line can be followed to the Gulfside Trail and then back to the hut. From the summit, the Air Line heads northeast along the ridge leading to Mt. John Quincy Adams. The top of this minor peak can be reached by scrambling over the great angular blocks on the summit ridge. On the southeast side of John Quincy Adams, not far below the summit, is an excellent exposure of folded schists of the Littleton formation.

The Air Line meets the Gulfside Trail (which is taken, right, back to the hut) near the head of King Ravine, a deep cirque that once contained an active valley glacier. King Ravine and Snyder Brook, immediately to the east, provide a most unusual contrast. The two adjacent valleys are parallel, both stretching for the same distance north from the northernmost ridge of the Presidentials. They both end at the same elevation at the Moose River. Nevertheless, U-shaped King Ravine obviously contained a valley glacier, whereas V-shaped Snyder Brook did not. One can only speculate on the reasons for this difference. King Ravine is northeast of the broad Nowell Ridge; snow-bearing winds from the southwest would dump prodigious quantities of snow into King Ravine, much as they do into Tuckerman Ravine today. Snyder Brook, however, is protected somewhat by the high summit of Mt. Adams. It is also to the lee of King Ravine for southwest winds. Thus, its valley likely received less snow than did King Ravine. The difference probably did not have to be much. Once a year-long snow cover developed in King Ravine, its heat balance would change to favor a buildup of snow and its eventual conversion into glacial ice. Snyder Brook, on the other hand, would melt its winter accumulation much the way Tuckerman Ravine does today.

This scenario depends on the general circulation patterns being the same during the period of valley glaciers as it is today. Climatological studies indicate that this is a reasonable assumption. It would be interesting to compare the precipitation patterns in the two drainages today. At any rate, the views down the two drainages from the Gulfside Trail provide an extraordinary contrast.

Star Lake Trail to the summit of Adams is just short of a mile, climbs 1,000 feet, and takes about 1 hour. The descent via the Air Line is slightly shorter and takes about 30 minutes.

Access to Adjacent Huts

Direct routes are available from Madison Spring Hut to Lakes of the Clouds Hut and Pinkham Notch Visitor Center. Both routes follow the Appalachian Trail.

Gulfside Trail to Lakes of the Clouds Hut. The trail begins at Snyder Brook between Mt. Madison and Mt. Adams, not more than 30 yards from the hut. After leading southwest through a patch of scrub, it aims to the right (north) of Mt. John Quincy Adams, and ascends a steep open slope. Near the top of this slope, it is joined from the right by the Air Line, with which it coincides for a few yards. From this point there is a fine view of Mt. Madison.

The path is now on the high plateau between the head of King Ravine and the summit of John Quincy Adams. The Air Line branches left toward Mt. Adams. Much of the Gulfside for the next half-mile is paved with carefully placed stones, placed by the builder, J. Rayner Edmands, and his group of imported laborers. The trail rises more steeply, and at 0.9 mile from the hut reaches a grassy lawn in the saddle between Mt. Adams and Mt. Sam Adams.

A gigantic cairn marks the intersection of a number of trails at this spot, known as Thunderstorm Junction. The summit of Mt. Sam Adams may be reached without a trail from this point; it affords a good view. (A cairned trail known as the White Trail runs from Thunderstorm Junction to the summit of Mt. Sam Adams and then follows its south ridge to a terminus where the Israel Ridge Path rejoins the Gulfside Trail about 100 yards south of Peabody Spring.

White-throated sparrows are common high on the ridges of the White Mountains. Betsy Fuchs.

The line of cairns is visible running roughly parallel to the Gulfside on the ridge to the north. It is more exposed than the Gulfside and should be avoided in bad weather.)

Continuing southwest from Thunderstorm Junction and beginning to descend, the Gulfside Trail is joined on the left by the Israel Ridge Path coming down from Lowe's Path, from which it diverges near the summit of Mt. Adams. The Gulfside Trail and the Israel Ridge Path coincide for 0.5 mile, passing Peabody Spring (unreliable) just to the right in a small grassy flat. A few yards beyond, more reliable water is found at the base of a conspicuous boulder just to the left of the path.

At 1.5 miles from the hut, the Israel Ridge Path diverges right. Near this junction in wet weather is a small pool called Storm Lake. The Gulfside turns a little to the left and approaches the edge of Jefferson Ravine, first passing Adams 5, a small peak just to the left of the trail. This part of the Gulfside was never graded. It is marked by cairns and keeps near the edge of the cliffs from which there are fine views into the gulf. Descending southwest along the narrow ridge that divides Jefferson Ravine from Castle Ravine and always leading toward Mt. Jefferson, it enters Edmands Col at 2.2 miles from the hut.

Edmands Col, between Mt. Adams and Mt. Jefferson, divides the Connecticut and Androscoggin watersheds. Its elevation is almost the same as that of the Madison-Adams col at the Parapet, and within 50 feet of that of the Clay-Jefferson col. There is a bronze tablet in memory of J. Rayner Edmands. About 30 yards south of the col is Gulfside Spring, which seldom fails.

South of Edmands Col, the Gulfside Trail ascends steeply southwest over rough rocks with Jefferson Ravine on the left. It passes flat-topped Dingmaul Rock, from which there is a good view down the gulf with Mt. Adams on the left. A few yards beyond, the Mt. Jefferson Loop branches right and leads in 0.2 mile to the summit of Mt. Jefferson (5,715 feet), from which it continues 0.3 mile to rejoin the Gulfside Trail at Monticello Lawn. The trip over the summit adds about 15 minutes walking time.

From the north Mt. Jefferson Loop junction, the Gulfside Trail turns southeast and rises less steeply. It crosses the Six Husbands Trail and soon reaches its greatest height on the eastern ridge of Mt. Jefferson at 5,370 feet. Curving southwest and descending a little, it crosses Monticello Lawn, a comparatively smooth, grassy plateau at an elevation of about 5,330 feet. Here the Mt. Jefferson Loop rejoins the Gulfside.

A short distance southwest of the lawn, the Cornice enters right from the Caps Ridge Trail. The Gulfside continues to descend south and southwest. From one point there is a view of the Sphinx to the left down the slope. Approaching the Clay-Jefferson col (Sphinx Col), the ridge and path turn more southerly. The Sphinx Trail branches left (east) into the Great Gulf through a grassy passage between ledges a few yards north of the col.

From the col, the Mt. Clay Loop diverges left while the graded Gulfside continues right around the summit. The Clay Loop is rough, but the views from the summit are impressive and worth the extra 15 minutes. Either way, there is a significant bedrock change shortly beyond the junction. Until now, the trail has led over bedrock from the upper part of the Littleton formation. The summit of Clay is formed of bedrock from the lower part, and the Boott member is exposed along the trails (see the cross section on pages 26–27). The route passes back onto the upper part of the Littleton formation just south of the summit of Mt. Clay and traverses it all the way to Lakes of the Clouds Hut.

From the north Clay Loop junction, the Gulfside runs south and rises gradually, slabbing the west side of Mt. Clay. In 0.3 mile, a loop leads a few yards down to the right to water. The loop path continues about 30 yards farther to reliable Greenough Spring, then rejoins the Gulfside farther up. The Gulfside continues its slabbing ascent. Just before it gains its highest point, one of the summits of Clay can be reached by a short climb to the left. Here the Jewell Trail from Marshfield enters from the right. The Gulfside swings southeast and descends slightly to the Clay-Washington col where the Mt. Clay Loop rejoins it from the left. This is just about the point where the trail recrosses onto the upper Littleton formation.

There is no water in this col. A little to the east is the edge of the Great Gulf with fine views of the eastern cliffs of Mt. Clay. The path continues southeast rising gradually toward the cog railway. About 200 yards from the col, the Westside Trail (direct route to the Lakes of the Clouds Hut) branches right and goes under the railroad.

(The Gulfside or the railway can be followed to the summit of Washington. From the summit, the Crawford Path is followed to its junction with the Westside Trail on the southwest side. The path over the top adds 700 feet of climbing and about 0.5 mile extra distance.)

The Westside Trail contours around the western side of Mt. Washington at an elevation of 5,600 feet and joins the Crawford Path in just less than a mile from the Gulfside. The Crawford Path heads southwestward below Bigelow Lawn, reaching a trail junction where the Tuckerman Crossover and the Camel Trail enter from the left. In a few yards, the trail passes to the left of the first of the lakes and quickly reaches the hut.

Total trail distance without going over the summits is about 6.8 miles and takes nearly 5 hours. Total climb is about 1,500 feet, half of which is gained in climbing from Madison Spring Hut to Thunderstorm Junction.

Pinkham Notch Visitor Center via the Appalachian Trail. Although the shortest route follows down the Madison Gulf Trail, the upper portion is very steep and rough and is not as scenic as the route that the AT follows. However, it does drop very quickly into the trees and would be the choice if a thunderstorm threatened.

The Appalachian Trail follows the Osgood Trail over Mt. Madison and down into the Great Gulf. The Osgood Trail leads down the crest of the Osgood Ridge into the timber and eventually reaches a trail junction where the AT branches right on the Osgood Cutoff. There is a spring at this junction. In 0.5 mile, the Osgood Cutoff makes a sharp left turn where it used to meet the Madison Gulf Trail (recently relocated). The next junction is with the Great Gulf Trail, which is followed, right, and descends to Parapet Brook, crossing it on a bridge. The Madison Gulf Trail now enters on the right, and the two trails coincide for a short distance. They descend to cross the West Branch of the Peabody River on a suspension bridge. The trail climbs the steep bank of the river, and in a few yards the Madison Gulf Trail diverges left (the Great Gulf Trail diverges right). This left branch is followed on a fairly level grade, crossing several brooks. It then ascends gradually to the Mt. Washington Auto Road just above the 2-mile marker. Just before reaching the road, a short trail branches left to Lowe's Bald Spot, a 5-minute walk to a fine viewpoint.

Just across the auto road, take the Old Jackson Road, which leads south, crossing through an old gravel pit and dropping slightly. Shortly, the Nelson Crag Trail leaves right. Several small brooks are crossed, and in a short distance the Raymond Path leaves right. The trail drops sharply, then climbs a short way to a height-of-land where George's Gorge Trail leaves left (east). (This junction may be incorrectly signed Liebeskind's Loop.) Now dropping steadily, it passes the junction with the Crew-Cut Trail, which diverges left. In about 0.3 mile, the Tuckerman Ravine Trail is met, which is followed, left, 50 yards to Pinkham Notch Visitor Center.

Total distance from Madison Spring Hut to Pinkham Notch Visitor Center is about 7.5 miles, and the route is downhill except for the 500 feet up and down Mt. Madison and a 500-foot gain between the Great Gulf Trail and the auto road. Time is about 4.5 hours.

▼ ▼ ▼

Self-Guided Nature Walk
Madison Spring Hut
by Jan M. Collins

Madison Hut sits on the edge of the alpine tundra. Red spruce, black spruce, and balsam fir are gnarled and stunted by the bitter winds, while specialized plants that colonized the area following the retreat of the glaciers cling tenaciously to the open rocky areas. Although these plants have special adaptations that allow them to survive weather extremes, they are not able to survive crushing footfalls.

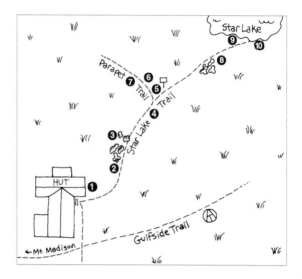

Please help preserve the fragile alpine environment by staying on the path.

Station One

Step outside the hut's front door and take a look at the walls. Notice some deep orange splotches all over the building. These are a lichen found in the Presidentials only on huts of stone and mortar. Calcium, found in limestone, and a necessary nutrient in the lichen's diet is rare in the Presidentials except as an ingredient in mortar. How did the lichen find its way to the hut? The nearest parent specimens could be miles away. Yet, lichens have a remarkable ability to self-propagate. A tiny fragment of a plant can be carried by the wind and if it lands in a suitable site, like a seam in the hut wall, a whole new organism will grow.

Station Two

As you leave the hut, turn left onto the Star Lake Trail. Before you enter the unbroken miniature forest, there is an island of vegetation on the left. The gnarled low-growing trees are called krummholz. The age of the krummholz balsam fir and dwarf birch in the island is estimated at 175 years. Like Japanese bonsai, they have been regularly pruned, creating miniature versions of trees that grow to over 40 feet at lower elevations. Unlike bonsai, the krummholz is shaped by the hand of nature, not by human hands. Buds on the windward side of the tree receive the brunt of the cold and ice and often die. Branches on the protected side survive, giving the tree a lopsided appearance.

Station Three

There will be a large vertical rock in the center of the trail as you begin a steep climb. On the bank to the left is an arrow-shaped rock sporting representatives from the three lichen categories. Crustose lichens are flat and hug the rock so tightly they cannot be peeled off. They can withstand the harshest of conditions, but often grow very slowly. One species, the apple-green map lichen, can be 1,000 years old when its diameter reaches 0.4 inch. You may be looking at some of the oldest living organisms in these mountains. Foliose lichens are dark green to brown and leafy. Fruticose lichens are represented here by the cup lichen, snow lichen, and reindeer moss lichen. Lichens are able to glean water from moist air or low clouds. They can photosynthesize at temperatures just above freezing, and they are able to survive long periods of darkness. Lichens also provide important microhabitats and contribute to soil formation by eroding the surface of rocks.

Station Four

As you continue up the trail, notice the rocks underfoot. It is difficult to imagine this place underwater, but 500 million years ago it was. Between 460 and 375 million years ago, the European continent collided with the North American continent. Sand, mud, and limestone were piled thousands of feet high. The heat and pressure resulting from the collision bonded some sedimentary rocks, transforming sandstone and shale into quartzite and schist, more resistant to weathering than the granite on the next ridge. Eventually, the continents began the process of separating and returning to their respective corners. Cracks in the bedrock allowed volcanoes to appear and magma bubbled up to the surface. The ridgeline of the Presidentials remains resistant to the forces of nature millions of years later. Even the glaciers did little to change their elevation, simply rounding off the rough edges. Large quartz rocks scattered on either side of this col are the remains of the magma from volcanic vents.

Station Five

When you reach the intersection of the Parapet Trail and the Star Lake Trail, look beneath and to the left of the sign. In the crevice between the two large rocks is a little plant called mountain sandwort. Without its blossoms it will look a bit like a moss because its leaves are tiny and close to the stem. The sandwort grows in soils that have been disturbed, so you may often see it along the edges or between rocks in the trail, safe from crushing footfalls. The leaf's limited surface means there is less area exposed to the drying forces of the ever-present winds. Mountain sandwort's showy white blossoms appear to be too big for such a small plant to support, but they are perfectly formed signals for attracting pollinators.

Station Six

Along the top of the larger of the two rocks are green waxy-leaved plants called mountain cranberry. Waxy leaves help the plant retain water. In addition, the plant's low growth keeps it out of the wind. It has a small pink flower in the shape of a nodding bell and begins blooming in late June. The berries appear in late August and are a deep red to maroon when ripe.

Station Seven

On the left side of the Parapet Trail you will find a shrubby plant called Labrador tea. If it is in bloom (early summer), at the end of the branch there will be a cluster of white flowers. Even it if is not in bloom, Labrador tea is easily identified. The underside of each leaf is covered with "fur." On this year's leaf the hairy underside may be white in color. On older leaves it will likely be golden brown. Why would a plant wear fur? One theory is that the hairs help the plant retain moisture by creating a dead-air space.

Station Eight

Return to the Star Lake Trail. Just after the last big patch of krummholz on your right, and before you get to Star Lake, you will enter a large patch of mountain avens with colonies on either side of the trail. In bloom its flowers look a lot like buttercups, a shiny bright yellow. Follow the flower stalk to the leaves at its base. They are semicircular and unusually large. Initially, so much exposed surface area seems an incongruous tactic for surviving the harsh drying winds of its alpine environment. Then we notice two things: first, the leaves are waxy; second, the plant is almost always found growing on the edge of wetlands or in moist depressions. What makes mountain avens so special? It is found in only two places in the world—here in the White Mountains and on an island in western Nova Scotia.

Station Nine

At Elephant Hump Rock on the north end of Star Lake, you will find cushions of diapensia all along the rock's length bordering the trail. Its leaves are thick and waxy like the mountain cranberry but so tightly growing that it is difficult to push a finger in between them and down to the ground. Its large white flowers bloom in early June and are quickly gone before the summer hiking season begins. Diapensia often grows in the most exposed areas of the alpine tundra. To survive the harsh conditions there, it must create its own protected environment. The leaves are so close-knit that wind does not penetrate through to the roots and they are protected from severe freezing. On sunny days, the temperature within the cushion of diapensia can be as much as 40°F warmer than the air only a few inches above it.

Station Ten

The banks along the right side of the trail just beyond Elephant Hump Rock are covered with a low-growing shrub called bog bilberry. It is a relative of the blueberry and has wonderfully sweet, dark blue berries which ripen at the end of August. Bilberry can be found growing in the protected lee of rocks and hillsides. Its leaves have a distinct reddish tinge along the margins.

Never pick or eat anything you cannot positively identify.

13
Carter Notch Hut

From the Hut Log: June 14, 1921

> I've swam in many a swimmin' pool.
>   I've bathed in bath-tubs, too.
> But the waters of yon Carter Lake,
>   I recommend to you
>
> **Frigidus Immersus**

ISOLATED Carter Notch, with its wild jumble of talus blocks, would seem an unlikely place for the third major hut-building effort of the AMC. But in 1904, 16 years after the Madison Spring refuge was built and three years after the Crawford Path refuge (Lakes of the Clouds), a small log cabin was built on the eastern shore of the larger of the two little lakes in Carter Notch. While the reasons for the first two were evident—shelter for above-timberline travelers—the reason for the Carter Notch camp is less clear. Carter Notch is, at 3,300 feet, well below timberline. And in 1904, it was not a particularly popular climbing area.

But as a hut site today, it has much to commend it. Carter Notch is the easternmost of the AMC huts. Stretching southwest from the notch lies the string of 4,000-foot peaks of the Wildcat Ridge. To the northeast lies the Carter-Moriah Range, the last of the 4,000-footers in the White Mountains as one heads toward the wild backcountry of Maine. Indeed, six of these high mountains are to be found between Wildcat E (4,041 feet) and Mt. Moriah (4,049 feet). And the notch has some of the finest scenery

Carter Notch Hut, built in 1914, is the oldest hut still in use.
AMC Collection.

in the region: the impressive pile of rocks that form the Rampart; the steep faces of Wildcat to the west and Carter Dome to the east; and two beautiful glacial tarns. The notch is well worth a visit for its own sake.

A second hut was built a short distance south of the lakes in 1914. It was a stone hut patterned after the second Madison Spring Hut. With a wooden roof and a cement floor, it measured 18 by 40 feet. The interior was divided into two rooms, the larger serving as a combination kitchen, dining room, and men's bunkroom, the smaller as a women's dormitory. The original hut was turned over to the Forest Service for use as living quarters for the Carter Dome fire-lookout crew. It was torn down a few years later.

The stone hut stands today and serves as the kitchen and dining room of the Carter Notch complex. It is the oldest hut in the system that is still in active use today.

The building was expanded in 1930 to add crew quarters. Three more buildings were added subsequently: two bunkhouses and a wash house. The interior of the main building was further remodeled in 1990 to improve the kitchen facilities. The present overnight capacity is 40, in very comfortable quarters. The hut is open all year with full service from early June to the beginning of September and with a caretaker in residence the rest of the year. Winter visitors usually snowshoe in via the Nineteen-Mile Brook Trail, although most of it can be negotiated on skis.

Geology

The most interesting geology in Carter Notch stems from the glacial and postglacial period. Although the notch had its present general shape prior to the ice age, continental glaciers deepened it and gave it the characteristic U-shape of heavily glaciated valleys. Since the retreat of the great ice sheet, frost action has split great chunks of rock from the slopes of Wildcat and Carter Dome and piled them in wild profusion on the floor of the notch. These are called the Rampart. (Some believe that the jumble of rocks was

The original Carter Notch Cabin, built in 1904. AMC Collection.

created in one massive rock avalanche.) From the lower bunkroom, you can see the great shallow bowl high on the slopes of Carter Dome from which many of these blocks have been riven. One such boulder that split off but has yet to make it to the bottom is Pulpit Rock.

The boulders are so large that they have formed numerous rock caves; some of these caves can be followed for some distance, mostly by crawling and wiggling. Many of the caverns between the rocks contain ice. This ice is so well protected from the melting action of sun and rain that it usually lasts well into the summer. It provides natural air conditioning for hot hikers.

The notch itself is carved into the upper part of the Littleton formation. Almost the entire range from Wildcat to the Androscoggin River and beyond is underlain by this formation.

Ecology

Carter Notch Hut lies in the elevational middle of the spruce-fir zone. Balsam fir and white birch abound in the vicinity. Just in front of the main building are several mountain ash trees (*Pyrus americana*). These small trees have compound leaves much like the true ash, but the main leaf stems are arranged alternately along the stem. In the true ash, the compound leaves are arranged in opposite pairs.

The moist woods in the hut vicinity often have a fine display of painted trillium (*Trillium undulatum*) if you visit the hut early in the summer.

Ecologically, the most interesting area is in and around the Rampart. Soil is very scant among the giant boulders and can support only a sparse and scrubby vegetation. The dominant tree is spruce, few of which are more than 20 feet tall. On the hut side of the Rampart are a number of ice caves, some of which feed cold air into narrow draws. The seasonal development of vegetation is retarded by several weeks because of the cold microclimate. Especially in the spring and early summer, you can find trees and shrubs that are just starting their vegetative growth, while only a few yards away, the same plant will be in full leaf. Because of the shorter growing season caused by this unusual microclimate, trees and shrubs also tend to be somewhat dwarfed. Often the boundary marking the edge of this little ecosystem is quite sharp, outlining in the vegetation the limits of the cold air drainage.

A self-guided nature walk is described at the end of the chapter.

Access to the Hut

The normal route of access to the hut is via the Nineteen-Mile Brook Trail from Route 16 north of Pinkham Notch. It is also possible to come up the Wildcat River Trail from the Carter Notch Road north of Jackson. Another alternative is to take the Wildcat Ridge Trail from Pinkham Notch.

Via Nineteen-Mile Brook Trail. The trail starts 1 mile north of the Mt. Washington Auto Road on Route 16, at a parking lot on the north side of Nineteen-Mile Brook. The graded path stays on the northeast side of the brook, climbing moderately through picturesque white birch trees. Just short of 2 miles from the highway, the Carter Dome Trail diverges left to Zeta Pass. Just beyond, the Nineteen-Mile Brook Trail crosses the brook on a bridge, and in 0.3 mile crosses another branch, also on a bridge. From here, the trail climbs toward the notch, staying some distance from the brook. Just before reaching the height-of-land,

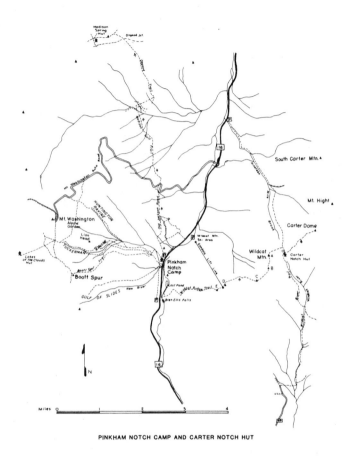

PINKHAM NOTCH CAMP AND CARTER NOTCH HUT

the trail steepens somewhat. At the highest point, the
Wildcat Ridge Trail enters from the right, and a side path
leads left a view of the Rampart. The Nineteen-Mile
Brook Trail heads down the slope toward the larger of the
two lakes, which it passes on the left. Here, the Carter-

Moriah Trail, part of the Appalachian Trail, diverges left. The Nineteen-Mile Brook Trail passes between the lakes, climbs slightly, and quickly reaches the hut.

Trail distance is 3.8 miles, and the total climb is 1,900 feet. Walking time is 3 hours.

Via Wildcat Ridge Trail from Pinkham Notch. This is a long, hard hike with many ups and downs. It is slippery and dangerous in wet weather. Even though it starts out at an elevation 500 feet higher than the Nineteen-Mile Brook Trail, the total climb is 3,000 feet as compared with 1,900 feet. The route is part of the Appalachian Trail and is marked with white paint blazes.

Across the road from the entrance to Pinkham Notch Visitor Center (free parking lot), the Lost Pond Trail is taken. This crosses on a bridge at the outlet of the beaver pond, then immediately turns right (south). Avoid a side trail on the left that leads upward to Square Ledge. The Lost Pond Trail follows the Ellis River, which is soon joined by the larger Cutler River, for 0.25 mile, then bears away from the river and climbs to Lost Pond on a moderate grade. After following the eastern shoreline, it descends slightly and joins the Wildcat Ridge Trail. This point is only about 0.1 mile from the highway near Glen Ellis Falls.

The Wildcat Ridge Trail leads east (left) from this junction and quickly starts climbing up the western ridge of Wildcat. Two open ledges are climbed, with good views of Mt. Washington. The trail continues steeply upward, crossing a number of ledges. At the top of a rocky knob, there is a spectacular view of Tuckerman Ravine and Mt. Washington. Above the knob, at a steep rise, there is a spring to the left (north) that is generally reliable. This is the last water before the hut.

The trail now climbs to summit E (4,041 feet), where the trail turns sharply north. It descends into a col (3,971 feet) at the upper terminal of the Wildcat Ski Area gondola. Passing behind the building, the trail climbs to summit D (4,062 feet), where there is a wooden lookout platform. The trail swings eastward around the north slope of D, then descends into Wildcat Col (3,775 feet). After passing a slightly higher col, the trail begins the long ascent to summit C (4,298 feet). There are good views from the top, but the best are to be had from a ledge 200 feet to the east of the trail.

The trail then loses about 150 feet of elevation in the C-B col, after which it makes the easy climb to the wooded B summit. After a drop of less than 100 feet into the next col, the trail climbs to the main summit at 4,422 feet. There is a viewpoint to the right of the trail. The route down from the summit is steep and meets the Nineteen-Mile Brook Trail at the col, which it follows, right, to the lakes and the hut.

Total distance from Pinkham Notch to Carter Notch Hut is 7 miles, and the elevation gain is 3,000 feet. Walking time is 6.5 hours.

Via Wildcat Gondola and Wildcat Ridge Trail. If the weather is hot and the thought of the long, arduous climb to the summit of Wildcat E turns you off, then consider riding the Wildcat Ski Area gondola to the ridge where the Wildcat Ridge Trail can be picked up. The gondolas run in the summer season. One-way tickets may be purchased for a modest fee. Cars may be parked free in the ski-area parking lot 2 miles north of Pinkham Notch Visitor Center.

This way, the total walking distance is 4.75 miles and the elevation gain is 1,000 feet, a saving of 2,000 feet. Walking time is 3.75 hours from the upper station.

Via Wildcat River Trail. The trail starts with the Bog Brook Trail, which begins at a small parking area on Carter Notch Road about 3.0 miles from Route 16B just west of its sharp turn at the crossing of Wildcat Brook. The Bog Brook Trail follows a dirt road (sign) past a camp and bears right off the road into the woods (blazed with blue diamonds) at the turnaround at the White Mountain National Forest boundary. Running nearly level, it crosses Wildcat Brook, another brook, and then the Wildcat River. In 60 yards the Wildcat River Trail continues straight ahead. The Wildcat River Trail emerges into a grassy opening with a view toward Carter Notch. Remaining on the east bank of Wildcat River, the trail crosses Bog Brook, and in 1 mile the Wild River Trail leaves right for Perkins Notch. The trail bears left, and in 0.3 mile crosses to the west bank of Wildcat River. It climbs moderately, then more steeply as it approaches the notch. The trail passes to the left side of the Rampart and soon reaches the hut.

Trail distance is 4.5 miles and total elevation gain is 1,600 feet. Walking time is 3.5 hours.

Day Hikes from Carter Notch Hut

The main point of interest in the vicinity is, of course, the Rampart, the spectacular jumble of house-size talus blocks. It is reached in a few minutes via the Wildcat River Trail. A few yards beyond the bunkhouses, various paths lead left to the edge of the Rampart. There is good, if rather cramped, spelunking and cool pools of air by the ice caves. As noted in the section on ecology, there is much of botanical interest here.

Carter Dome via Carter-Moriah Trail. The Carter-Moriah Trail begins at the Nineteen-Mile Brook Trail at the larger lake and ascends the steep lower slope of the dome. Just beyond the steep part, a trail leads right to Pulpit Rock, which can be climbed (but with great caution). As the main trail continues, the ascent becomes less steep. The top is open and excellent views are to be had.

Trail distance is 1.2 miles, and the elevation gain is 1,600 feet. Walking time is 1.5 hours.

Wildcat Mtn. via Wildcat Ridge Trail. At the height-of-land just north of the Carter lakes, the Wildcat Ridge Trail diverges left from the Nineteen-Mile Brook Trail. The Wildcat Ridge Trail ascends steeply to the main summit of Wildcat. The East View, a ledge with excellent views of the notch, is reached by a side path left a few yards beyond the summit.

Trail distance is 1.8 miles, and the elevation gain is 1,200 feet. Walking time is a little over 1 hour.

Access to Adjacent Huts

Both Pinkham Notch Visitor Center and Madison Spring Hut are readily reached from Carter Notch.

Pinkham Notch Visitor Center via the Wildcat Ridge Trail. The Nineteen-Mile Brook Trail is followed north from the hut to the height-of-land where the Wildcat Ridge Trail branches left (west). The climb to the main summit is steep. At the summit (4,422 feet), a sign indicates the route south along the ridge. After dropping 150 feet into the col, the trail climbs about 50 feet to summit B (4,330 feet). Again dropping about 150 feet into the next col, it ascends summit C (4,298 feet), then begins a longer descent into Wildcat Col, the lowest point on the ridge (3,775 feet). A climb of about 300 feet in elevation brings you to the D summit (4,062 feet), on which there is a low platform with good views. In a few yards, the upper terminal of the Wildcat gondola is reached. The gondola operates in summer and may be taken to the base, about 1 mile north of Pinkham Notch Visitor Center.

For the hardy ones, the Wildcat Ridge Trail continues upward, gaining about 80 feet in elevation before reaching summit E (4,041 feet). Here the trail turns right (west) and descends over a rocky prominence to two ledges. At the lower edge the path down is at the right of the viewpoint.

After the trail has leveled off at the bottom, the Lost Pond Trail branches right (north) and is followed to Pinkham Notch Visitor Center.

Trail distance is 7 miles, and the elevation gain is about 1,500 feet. Walking time is 3 hours to the gondola and 5.5 hours for the entire route.

Madison Spring Hut via Nineteen-Mile Brook Trail and Osgood Trail. The Nineteen-Mile Brook Trail is taken to Route 16, which is followed 0.5 mile north to the Great Gulf parking area on the west side of the highway. (Note that the Nineteen-Mile Brook Link has been abandoned.)

The Great Gulf Trail descends from the parking lot and crosses the Peabody River on a bridge. In 0.3 mile, the Great Gulf Link from Dolly Copp Campground enters from the right. The Great Gulf Trail now turns sharp left and follows an old logging road close to the bank of the West Branch of the Peabody River, then diverges southwestward until the Osgood Trail junction is reached at 1.8 miles from the start.

The Osgood Trail proceeds northwestward (right), then curves northward to the junction with the Osgood Cutoff which comes in from the left. (A spur trail right leads in 100 yards to Osgood Campsite and a spring with the last sure water.) Continuing northward, the trail climbs on a increasingly steep grade to the crest of Osgood Ridge. It now follows on the crest and is marked by cairns. Within a half-mile of the summit of Mt. Madison, the Daniel Webster–Scout Trail from Dolly Copp Campground enters from the right at Osgood Junction. The Osgood Trail continues to the summit of Mt. Madison and on down to Madison Spring Hut. This involves a 500-foot climb to the summit and equal descent to the hut.

For an easier route, one that is recommended especially in bad weather, take the Parapet Trail, left, from Osgood Junction. This heads west more or less on a contour, through partly open tundra, partly scrub woods, to Star Lake, at the col between Madison Gulf and Snyder Brook. The Madison Gulf Trail enters from the left, and the two routes join with the Star Lake Trail to reach the hut in 0.3 mile.

▼ ▼ ▼

A Self-Guided Nature Walk
Carter Notch
by Ray Welch

Station One

Start your walk here at the outlet of the upper of the lakes at Carter Notch. Notice that the water is very clear and the rocks and sand are easily seen on the bottom—even out to a considerable depth. There are also not many water plants. A nice, clean-looking lake for a swim. And stocked with trout. Lakes like this are called oligotrophic ("little-feeding")

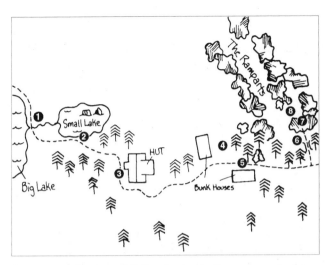

because nutrients needed for plant growth are scarce in these pure waters—so few plants are seen. But plants are the basis for animal food chains. What feeds the trout? They dine on aquatic insects that feed on plant debris washed or blown in from the lush surrounding forest. They also prey on land insects that unwisely visit the water surface.

Station Two

Walk back toward the hut to the shore of the smaller lake. You started at the flowing outlet of the upper lake. Look around. You'll notice that this lake does not have a visible outlet. Depending on how much rain has fallen, lake level may be up or down and if down, you can see "tub marks" on lake rocks marking high-water levels. The lake has no outflowing stream, but it does have a drain, through a leaky bottom. The rockfall that produced the Rampart blocked the end of the valley to the south, and while it made a reasonable dam, it was not perfect. And so the lake oozes invisibly away, to reemerge in the valley to the south as springs that seem to be the headwaters of the Wildcat River. But the real and secret headwaters lie before you.

Station Three

Walk back to the main hut. As you go uphill you pass through a young forest of conifers, mostly balsam fir. See how gloomy it is as you pass under them, and how little undergrowth there is to your right, because of the skimpy amount of sun that struggles down through the branches above. But pause at the Nineteen-Mile Brook Trail sign by the hut. The clearing for the hut lets sunlight all the way to the ground, and the site responds by supporting a rich group of low plants. Opposite the hut door are two kinds of deciduous plants with fernlike leaves, one a tree, the other a shrub. The tree is mountain ash and the shrub is mountain elderberry. Although they look similar, and even bear red fruits in favorable seasons (not quite at the same time), they are not related. Nature follows many similar paths, and even quite distant relatives can end up looking much alike.

Station Four

Go on to the bunkhouses and stand in the clearing in front of the first you come to. When you face it, the cliffs of Wildcat rise steeply up on your left. These may look like fearsome places to get to, but if you have wings it's no problem. In the cracks and crevices of these cliffs, or in the caves among the fallen rocks, dwell little brown bats that emerge in summer dusk to dart and flutter after insect prey. Come back then and you may see them. On the rock ledges far above, American ravens, rare elsewhere in the East, raise their young, safe from predators. The raven is a member of the crow family, looking like one, but much larger. Their voices are often heard before you spot them—hoarse squawks and cries.

Station Five

Go on a little to the next bunkhouse and stand on the trail by its far corner. On your immediate left is a great, jagged rock sunk in the ground among the trees. At first glance only a barren boulder, a moment's scrutiny shows you it is covered with life. And, indeed, it is slowly being overwhelmed and smothered. On the steeper sides of the rock are colonies of moss (dark green, soft patches) and lichen (grayish, scaly crusts) that break down into humus that can collect in patches, along with weathered rock debris, into soil. On the south side a young tree has established itself in a crack. It will take a long time, but the soft vegetation will finally conquer the hard rock.

Station Six

Go on another hundred feet or so until the trail to the Rampart leaves on the left. From here on the footing is rocky and uncertain. Take care! You cross a simple log bridge over a crevasse and see before you a very large boulder slab that rises up to block your view. Stop just where the trail starts to climb the rock. On your left is a thicket of small evergreens. Many people call anything with needles a "pine." But pines have their needles in groups along the twig. Conifer needles are not clustered, but are all up and down the twig. One of these conifers has flat needles, soft when you firmly grasp a branchlet. It is balsam fir. The other has roundish needles, prickly when you "shake hands." This is a spruce. There are two species: black spruce, with bluish-green needles and small (0.5 inch) cones, and red spruce, with dark-green needles and larger cones (1 to 1.5 inches), which is more common. Can you see both of the species here?

Station Seven

Climb onto the great rock just ahead and stop on its highest part. All around lies a chaotic and dismaying landscape—the Rampart. If you look to your left you can see that the silhouette of Carter Notch is U-shaped. During the ice age, glaciers pushed through here and rounded the valley floor and then steepened the side slopes of Wildcat and Carter Dome into cliffs. When the glaciers melted some time later, the upper part of Carter collapsed in a titanic rockfall. You can still see the great scar and few huge blocks marooned part way down. This was the avalanche that created the lakes where we began. The lichens that coat the rocks and the sparse soil patches scattered among them tell us the event occurred long ago. If you should choose to pick your way out across the Rampart you will be struck continually by the power of the event that in a few seconds could plunge down these chunks, changing the notch forever.

Station Eight

Our formal walk soon ends a few feet farther on. Carefully step down the other side of the slab to where low vegetation grows in the scanty soil patches. Although these plants may seem scruffy and nondescript, a closer look shows you that these species are absent from the surrounding woods. The thin soil, the relentless winds—note the wind-flagged trees—and the sunny aspect (when the sun is out) make this spot like the mountaintops, and mountain plants are found here. There is mountain cranberry, a creeping shrub with tiny, dark-green, lustrous leaves; needle-leafed crowberry, looking almost like a dwarf spruce; low, tangled clumps of brownish-green Iceland lichen; and shrubby Labrador tea, whose simple dark-green leaves have densely woolly undersides. You stand on a bit of near-tundra, far from mountaintops, born of a mountain's fall.

Sources of Information

Guidebooks

The standard trail guide is the *AMC White Mountain Guide,* published by the Appalachian Mountain Club, 5 Joy Street, Boston, MA 02108. The *AMC Guide to Mt. Washington and the Presidential Range* contains trail descriptions excerpted from the full guide plus additional information relating specifically to hiking in the Presidentials.

For the Pinkham Notch area, see *Short Hikes & Ski Trips around Pinkham Notch,* by Linda B. Allen and Bradford Washburn, published by the AMC. This includes an excellent map of the area at a scale of 1:5,000.

The Franconia Notch region is described in detail in *Franconia Notch: An In-depth Guide* by Diane M. Kostecke and published by the Society for the Protection of New Hampshire Forests. It includes information on both the human and the natural history of the notch.

Randolph Paths, published by the Randolph Mountain Club, Randolph, NH 03570, contains detailed information on the trails of the northern peaks and slopes of the Presidentials.

Maps

The maps that are included with the AMC guidebooks can also be purchased separately. Most of them are available printed on tyvek for a small extra charge. A large-scale map of the *Randolph Valley and the Northern Peaks of the Mt. Washington Range,* published by the Randolph Mountain Club, is available on plain paper or tyvek.

But the most comprehensive map for hikers in the Presidentials is *Mt. Washington and the Heart of the Presi-*

dential Range, New Hampshire, at a scale of 1:20,000, first published in 1988 by the AMC. The surveyor and compiler was Bradford Washburn and the basic data were from aerial photos taken by two Swiss firms. It is a must for anyone hiking the region. Be advised, however, that some trails have changed since 1988. The *White Mountain Guide* maps are more up-to-date.

Topographical maps covering the area of this guide have been published by the U.S. Geological Survey and are available from the Branch of Distribution, USGS, 1200 South Eads Street, Arlington, VA 22202, and from many outdoor-equipment suppliers. They are published in two series: 7.5-minute quadrangles at a scale of 1:24,000; and 15-minute quadrangles at a scale of 1:62,500. Unfortunately, maps of both series must be obtained to cover the area included in this guide. *Franconia* (7.5-minute, 1967) includes the area around Lonesome Lake Hut and Greenleaf Hut. *South Twin Mountain* (7.5-minute, 1967) covers the area around Galehead Hut. Zealand Falls Hut and Mizpah Spring Hut are on the *Crawford Notch* (15-minute, 1946). The *Mt. Washington* quadrangle (15-minute, 1935) includes Lakes of the Clouds Hut, Madison Spring Hut, and Pinkham Notch. Carter Notch Hut is on the *Carter Dome* quadrangle (7.5-minute, 1970). The area around Pinkham Notch is covered by the *North Conway* quadrangle (15-minute, 1942).

Natural History

The indispensable guide to the alpine flora of the high peaks of the White Mountains is the *AMC Field Guide to Mountain Flowers of New England,* published by the AMC. The pamphlet *Alpine Zone of the Presidential*

Range by L. C. Bliss, published by the author, is available from the AMC. *Trees and Shrubs of Northern New England,* by Frederic L. Steele and Alvin R. Hogdon, published by the Society for the Protection of New Hampshire Forests, covers the woody vegetation of the mountains and valleys.

The geology of the White Mountains has been exhaustively studied. Unfortunately, most of the publications resulting from these studies are out of print. The publications currently available (from the New Hampshire Department of Resources and Economic Development, P.O. Box 856, Concord, NH 03301) include: *Map of the Geology of New Hampshire* (GEO-44); *Geology of the Gorham Quadrangle,* Bulletin No. 6; and *Geology of the Crawford Notch Quadrangle.* Others that have been published by the state of New Hampshire and that may be available in local libraries include: *The Geology of the Mt. Washington Quadrangle; Geology of the Franconia Quadrangle; The Geology of New Hampshire, Part I—Surficial Geology,* and *Part II—Bedrock Geology.*

The weather and climate of the mountain region are treated in interesting fashion in David Ludlum's *The Country Journal New England Weather Book,* published by Houghton Mifflin. *Weathering the Wilderness: The Sierra Club Guide to Practical Meteorology* by William E. Reifsnyder and published by Sierra Club Books, contains additional information on the climate of the White Mountains for hikers and skiers.

Index

About the Author

WILLIAM E. REIFSNYDER is Professor Emeritus of Forest Meteorology and Biometeorology at Yale University's School of Forestry and Environmental Studies. He held a joint appointment in the Department of Epidemiology and Public Health in the School of Medicine, and also served as Senior Research Scientist at the Environmental Research Laboratories of the National Oceanic and Atmospheric Administration in Boulder, Colorado.

Reifsnyder is Editor-in-Chief of the international journal, *Agricultural and Forest Meteorology,* and the author of more than 100 articles published in scholarly and scientific journals. He is the author of *Weathering the Wilderness,* a book on weather and climate for outdoor recreationists, and also written four outdoor books published by the Sierra Club and the Appalachian Mountain Club.

Reifsnyder attended Syracuse University and New York University, receiving a BS degree in meteorology from the latter institution in 1944. He received a Master of Forestry degree from the University of California, Berkeley, in 1949; and a PhD degree from Yale University in 1954.

His late wife, the former Marylou Bishop of San Francisco, was an artist and author of children's books; and co-authored a hiking guide, *Adventuring in the Alps* (Sierra Club).

About the AMC

THE Appalachian Mountain Club is where recreation and conservation meet. Our 55,000 members have joined the AMC to pursue their interests in hiking, canoeing, skiing, walking, rock climbing, bicycling, camping, kayaking, and backpacking, and—at the same time—to help safeguard the environment in which these activities are possible.

Since it was founded in 1876, the Club has been at the forefront of the environmental protection movement. By cofounding several of New England's leading environmental organizations, and working in coalition with these and many more groups, the AMC has influenced legislation and public opinion.

Volunteers in each chapter lead hundreds of outdoor activities and excursions and offer introductory instruction in backcountry sports. The AMC education department offers members and the public a wide range of workshops, from introductory camping to the intensive Mountain Leadership School taught on the trails of the White Mountains.

The most recent efforts in the AMC conservation program include river protection, Northern Forest Lands policy, support for the American Heritage Trust, Sterling Forest (NY) preservation, and support for the Clean Air Act.

The AMC's research department focuses on the forces affecting the ecosystem, including ozone levels, acid rain and fog, climate change, rare flora and habitat protection, and air quality and visibility.

The AMC Volunteer Trails Program is active throughout the AMC's twelve chapters and maintains over 1,200 miles of trails, including 350 miles of the Appalachian Trail. Under the supervision of experienced leaders, hundreds of volunteers spend from one afternoon to two weeks working on trail projects.

At the AMC headquarters in Boston and at Pinkham Notch Visitor Center in New Hampshire, the bookstore and information center stock the entire line of AMC publications, as well as other trail and river guides, maps, reference materials, and the latest articles on conservation issues. Guidebooks and other AMC gifts are available by mail order (AMC, P.O. Box 298, Gorham NH 03581), or call toll-free 800-262-4455. Also available from the bookstore or by subscription is *Appalachia,* the country's oldest mountaineering and conservation journal.

Begin a New Adventure—Join the AMC

We invite you to join the Appalachian Mountain Club and share the benefits of membership. Every member receives *AMC Outdoors*, the membership magazine that, ten times a year, brings you not only news about environmental issues and AMC projects, but also listings of outdoor activities, workshops, excursions, and volunteer opportunities. Members also enjoy discounts on AMC books, maps, educational workshops, and guided hikes, as well as reduced fees at all AMC huts and lodges in Massachusetts and New Hampshire.

To join, send a check for $40 for an adult membership, or $65 for a family membership to AMC, Dept. S7, 5 Joy Street, Boston MA 02108; or call 617-523-0636 for payment by Visa or MasterCard.   S7